P9-CCL-874

"This introduction to depression places the disease in the context of women's interpersonal relationships, simply and methodically underscoring the correlation between a woman's formative connections with her parents, her romantic relationships as an adult, and her emotional well-being and sense of self.... [*A Secret Sadness*] encourages women suffering from depression to undergo therapy, and information about treatment options, with a brief mention of antidepressants, rounds out the book. Readers are left with an encouraging mantra: 'Remember that our lives don't change; we change our lives.'"

—Publishers Weekly, January 2006

"*A Secret Sadness* is a map of what is known about the kinds of relationships that contribute to women's depression. Whiffen also discusses the influence of hormones, genetics, stressful events, losses, and gender roles in depression. The book is a compelling read and is jammed with sound, useful information—it provides a straightforward, well-informed answer to a very complex question: Can your relationships make you depressed?"

—Janice Thompson, Ph.D., registered psychologist in private practice in West Vancouver, BC

"An excellent book. Whiffen's writing style is very clear and her clinical perspective is supported by solid science. An excellent adjunct to psychotherapy for women with depression."

—Marcia McCoy, Ph.D., C.Psych.

"Blending research with clinical wisdom, Whiffen shows how the very relationships that sustain us can be the source of emotional insecurity and crippling depression. This book is essential reading for anyone who works with women facing depression."

—Sue Johnson, Ed.D., professor of psychology at the University of Ottawa and author of *Hold Me Tight*

a secret sadness

the hidden
relationship patterns
that make women
depressed

VALERIE E. WHIFFEN, PH.D.

New Harbinger Publications, Inc.

Publisher's Note

This publication is designed to provide accurate and authoritative information in regard to the subject matter covered. It is sold with the understanding that the publisher is not engaged in rendering psychological, financial, legal, or other professional services. If expert assistance or counseling is needed, the services of a competent professional should be sought.

Distributed in Canada by Raincoast Books

Copyright © 2009 by Valerie E. Whiffen
New Harbinger Publications, Inc.
5674 Shattuck Avenue
Oakland, CA 94609
www.newharbinger.com

Cover design by Amy Shoup; Text design by Michele Waters-Kermes; Acquired by Melissa Kirk; Edited by Elisabeth Beller

All Rights Reserved

Printed in the United States of America

Paperback ISBN: 978-157224-692-8

The Library of Congress has cataloged the hardcover edition as:

Whiffen, Valerie E.
  A secret sadness : the hidden relationship patterns that make women depressed / Valerie E. Whiffen.
      p. cm.
  ISBN-13: 978-1-57224-469-6
  ISBN-10: 1-57224-469-0
  1. Depression in women. 2. Depressed persons—Family relationships. I. Title.
RC537.W435 2006
616.85'270082—dc22

2006031467

11 10 09

10 9 8 7 6 5 4 3 2 1

First Printing

This book is dedicated to Julian and Niall,
for having faith in me.

contents

acknowledgments

There are many people whose assistance and support I would like to acknowledge.

Among my colleagues at the University of Ottawa, I would like to thank Sue Johnson for teaching me how to do couple therapy ten years ago and for holding my hand over many a cup of "gnat-pee" tea; Caroline Andrew, who as the Dean of Social Sciences gave me her unwavering support; and Al Mahrer for laughing at my jokes and encouraging me to keep writing.

I also would like to thank Kidest Mengistu, my Research Coordinator for the past three years, for dropping everything to run over to the library to photocopy an article for me and for taking such good care of my research that I could give all my attention to this book.

I would like to thank the graduate students who have taken my courses over the years and who have allowed me to supervise their clinical work. I have learned a great deal from their intelligent questions and from the skill and insight they bring to their clinical work. I am especially indebted to Trevor Deck, Marlene Best, Natasha Demidenko, Dalit Weinberg, Hannah Davis, Marcia McCoy, Leanne Campbell, Veronica Kallos-Lilly, Gordon Josephson, and Jan Thompson.

Finally, I would like to thank my many clients over the years. I hope I've been true to your experiences.

introduction

Women are twice as likely as men to experience depression (Nolen-Hoeksema 1990). This has been shown in both developed and developing countries around the world. One in four women will experience at least one episode of depression in her lifetime. Some women experience many episodes.

In childhood, the rates of depression among boys and girls are roughly the same. But something happens when girls go through puberty. The rate of girls' depression suddenly shoots up, and it stays higher until late old age (Jorm 1987). Many theories have been put forward to explain this fact but none is universally accepted.

In this book, I explore what it is about the lives of girls and women that puts them at risk for depression. I bring together the research on gender roles and the research on depression to show why women become depressed and what they can do about it.

WHY ARE WOMEN AT RISK?

A large body of psychological research tells us something that many of us already know: girls and women place a lot of importance on their closest relationships. Our parents, relatives, romantic partners and spouses, children, and friends are central to our lives. We value our relationships with these people immensely, and we feel good about ourselves when we are able to create relationships with them that are warm, intimate, and loving. Our need to do so is healthy and adaptive. When our most intimate relationships are good, they protect us from becoming depressed. But when they are riddled with conflict and emotional insecurity, they actually increase our risk for depression.

The relationship a woman creates with her romantic partner or spouse in particular is a key determinant of how good she feels about herself and how emotionally well she is. A woman who feels supported and cared for by her romantic partner may go through difficult times in her life, but she is generally able to ride out such times, even to grow from them. Depression occurs when a woman is alone and isolated or when she is involved in a romantic relationship that leaves her feeling uncared for and inadequate.

This romantic partner does not have to be a man. Very little research has been done on romantic relationships between women, but there is every reason to believe that much of what we know about married women also applies to women in same-sex relationships. I don't focus specifically on same-sex relationships in this book, but much of what I have to say is relevant to lesbian and bisexual women as well as heterosexual women.

HIDDEN RELATIONSHIP PATTERNS

Girls and women who are vulnerable to depression often grow up in families where they are ignored or rejected only to enter romantic relationships and marriages where they feel unsupported and unloved. Why does this happen?

Relationships in our first families shape our beliefs and expectations for later close relationships, most importantly with romantic partners but also with close friends and children. What we learn about ourselves and about loving in our first families is generalized to these later relationships. Often we are unaware of what we have learned. Our beliefs are played out in the patterns we create in our closest relationships, but they are often hidden from us. Our best friend may be able to see the patterns over the years, and the people we interact with certainly feel their effects, but we are blind. My goal is to help you see the hidden relationship patterns that may be making or keeping you depressed.

WHO THIS BOOK IS FOR

I wrote this book both for the women who experience depression and for the people who love and want to help them. My goal is to help you understand the interpersonal context in which depression occurs and how this context can trap women in a revolving door of disappointment and unhappiness.

I strongly believe that women need professional help to stop feeling depressed. However, you can read this book as a self-help book. At the end of each chapter, I provide a set of questions for you to ask yourself, which I hope will help you to apply the chapter material to your own experience. While you read the book, you might want to keep a journal where you write down your answers and other thoughts you have. If you decide to seek psychotherapy, your answers to these questions could help you figure out what you want to talk about.

WHO AM I?

I am a professor in the Clinical Psychology program at the University of Ottawa in Canada. I have researched the causes of depression for more than twenty years. I have taught courses, supervised the clinical training of graduate students, and treated depressed women for almost as long. This book is about how I understand women's depression.

I had many reasons for writing it. I am always frustrated by the poor information that is available to women about their depression. I wanted to write a book that would give depressed women and their families accurate information about the causes and consequences of depression. The information in this book is based on research and my clinical experiences. Whenever possible, I found recent papers that reviewed the research literature on the topics I discuss. These papers provide basic information about the topic and summarize the existing research literature. At the end of the book, you'll find a reference list of these and other sources. If you want more information, you should be able to find these books and review papers at any university library.

Most of the books that have been written for depressed people do not talk specifically about women's depression or the factors that might be unique to women. Yet men and women experience the world and close relationships in very different ways. I wanted to write a book that specifically examined the causes of women's depression from the perspective of their close relationships.

Finally, I wanted to pass on what I have learned, not just from doing research on depression but from the many depressed women with whom I have worked. These women opened their hearts to me. They did so to help themselves, but they also helped me. They gave me insight into why women get depressed and how they make themselves better that I couldn't have grasped if I had read thousands of research papers. Now I would like to help you. It is my hope that in reading this book, those of you who are depressed will come to understand the origins of your depression. With that knowledge, I hope you will find the help you need to exit the revolving door for the last time.

CHAPTER 1

the black dog of depression

Everyone has a period in her life when she feels down in the dumps and discouraged. Misfortune is a normal part of life. Even in a life filled with success, occasional disappointment is inevitable. Most of us ride out these bad times. In small doses, these experiences even help us grow. But sometimes we can't bounce back. Maybe we can't get up again because life has hit us too often or too hard. Maybe we find ourselves stuck in a painful situation that we can't escape.

It is at these times of our lives that we are likely to experience depression.

COMMON COLD OR BLACK DOG?

Researchers are fond of calling depression the "common cold" of emotional distress. They want to draw attention to the fact that depression is common in developed regions like the United States, Canada, Australia, the United Kingdom, and Europe. Although no one is quite sure why, people are more likely to become depressed now than they were a generation ago.

Depression may be common, but it is no cold. The comparison to a short-lived illness that for most people is no more than an inconvenience does not tell the truth about depression. Depression is extremely painful. Depressed people literally experience heaviness and crippling pain, usually in their hearts. They carry this pain with them throughout the day. Even their dreams are painful.

Unlike the common cold, depression isn't over in a week. Winston Churchill, who suffered from periods of depression throughout his life, called it a "black dog" that gripped him in its powerful jaws and would not let go. Without treatment, people are depressed on average for nine months before they start to feel better (Hollon et al. 2005). Clinicians often see people who have been depressed for years.

Worse, depression is like the cat in the kids' song: it keeps coming back. Most people don't experience a single episode. In fact, the risk of depression increases with every episode experienced (Belsher and Costello 1988). Those who are prone to depression may struggle their whole lives, feeling unhappy and dissatisfied without knowing why. Or they may have peaks and valleys, times they feel better punctuated by times they feel much worse.

Adults who are prone to depression spend about 15 percent of their lives depressed (Judd et al. 1998). That's almost two months out of every year. For another eight months they have symptoms that aren't severe enough or don't last long enough to be classified as depression, but these symptoms still interfere with their ability to enjoy life and feel good about themselves. That leaves only two months of the year when the people who are prone to depression actually feel okay.

Depression is nothing like the common cold. For many people, it is more like a severe, chronic illness with good times and bad, like diabetes or rheumatism. Like these diseases, depression is not due to a virus that temporarily invades our bodies. It is an illness that stems from an underlying process that has gone seriously wrong.

WHAT IT MEANS TO BE DEPRESSED

The symptoms of depression run the gamut from the physical to the psychological and emotional. You probably know you're depressed when you feel sad or down most of the time, but sadness isn't the only bad feeling a depressed woman can have. You may feel angry or easily irritated. You may feel flat, empty, or numb. You may feel that everything you do is too much trouble. If you feel this way most of the time, you could be depressed even if you're not aware of feeling sad.

A number of other symptoms are associated with depression. These include:

- Increased or decreased appetite

- Weight gain or weight loss without dieting

- Increased need for sleep

- Insomnia (i.e., you can't fall asleep or you wake up in the middle of the night or for the final time much earlier than usual)

- Fatigue

- Feelings of restlessness and agitation or extreme lethargy

- Trouble with concentration, difficulty making decisions, or being easily distracted

- Hopelessness, discouragement, pessimism about the future

- Feelings of inadequacy

- Self-blame and guilt

- Loss of interest in activities you normally enjoy

- Wishing you were dead and having some idea about how you might commit suicide

If a woman experiences several of these symptoms every day for at least two weeks, she is considered *clinically depressed*. Clinical depression is serious enough to need treatment. However, most people do not receive it. In Canada, where health care is accessible to everyone, only about 5 percent of the people who are clinically depressed seek and receive treatment (Hunsley, Lee, and Aubry 1999).

If you feel down, angry, or numb most of the time and you often experience several of the other symptoms, you may be clinically depressed. You may want to consult a physician or mental health professional about these symptoms.

The Psychological Symptoms

Tim Beck is a psychiatrist who has written widely on the subject of depression. He describes the psychological symptoms of depression as involving what he calls the *negative cognitive triad*: all-encompassing negative thoughts about the self, the world, and the future (Beck 1967; Beck et al. 1979).

What do we mean when we say that depressed people feel bad about themselves? They feel inadequate. They feel ashamed. They believe that no matter how hard they try they will never be good enough. They blame themselves when things go wrong. Often this self-blame is subtle. For instance, they may feel that they must make sure everyone in their family is happy. At other times the self-blame isn't rational. For instance, one depressed woman believed that all of the bad things in the world—from child abuse to global warming—were happening because she was a bad person.

The depressed person's negative view extends to the world around her. Depressed people suspect other people don't really like them; they anticipate criticism and rejection. Some depressed people protect themselves from criticism and rejection by keeping others at a distance. They tell themselves that they don't need close relationships and that they prefer to be alone and self-sufficient. The loneliness they sometimes feel is less painful than being hurt by someone close to them. Other depressed people constantly run after others, seeking approval, comfort, and reassurance that they are loved. This behavior can make others angry and drive them away, confirming the depressed person's fear that they will be rejected. Depressed people often believe that others expect them to be perfect. They believe no one will love them if they are flawed, which leads them to set high standards for themselves that are impossible to meet.

In light of the picture depressed people have of themselves and the people around them, it is not surprising that they have difficulty imagining a better future. They see themselves trapped in difficult situations over which they have little control. They feel helpless to change their lives. Many depressed people keep struggling to find happiness despite these feelings of discouragement. However, for some depressed people, hopelessness becomes so great that they consider taking their lives and may even have a plan for doing so. Although not everyone who considers suicide is depressed, suicide is one of the tragic outcomes of severe, repeated episodes of depression.

The Physical Symptoms

Depression also involves physical symptoms, including changes in appetite, energy levels, and sleep habits. Physical functions are *dysregulated*, which means that there is either an increase or a decrease compared to what is normal for that person. So a depressed person could sleep an extra three hours a day or be up half the night with insomnia—sometimes both. She could eat constantly or never feel hungry. She could feel so lethargic that she can't move or so restless that she can't sit still. With these physical changes come mental changes. Depressed people have great difficulty thinking through simple tasks or problems. A depressed woman can take hours to make choices about what to cook for dinner then change her mind halfway through preparing the meal. Even simple acts can be overwhelming. One depressed woman couldn't figure out how to open the curtains in her bedroom without putting down her baby, who she feared would roll off the bed. So she sat on the bed until her husband came home from work.

The Core Feeling Is Sadness

Above all, depression is an intensely emotional experience in which the core feeling is sadness. Often this sadness is expressed in constant, uncontrollable weeping. I use the word "weeping" deliberately to describe the constant welling and spilling of tears that many depressed people experience. Crying can be triggered by anything: a movie, a book, a painful memory. When we are sad, the world seems to torment us with constant reminders of our sorrow. At some point this sadness may become unbearable, and the depressed person seems to shut down emotionally. She experiences an overwhelming sense of emptiness or numbness.

Sadness is a normal human emotion. It is the emotion we feel when we lose something we value like an important relationship, when we fail to achieve an important goal, when we are extremely disappointed, or when we are rejected, criticized, or betrayed by someone we love or admire. Sadness can be profound, as it is after the death of a loved one. However, depression is not just sadness that is especially intense or doesn't go away. In part, depression is different from sadness because it changes the way we feel about ourselves. When we are depressed, we feel we aren't good enough or that we are to blame for our problems. When sadness changes the way we feel about ourselves, we are on the road to depression.

Emotions—even ones that feel bad—are normal and adaptive. Emotions have what are called *signal functions*. Emotions allow us to identify situations and people as the sources of pleasure and pain. When someone makes us laugh and feel good about ourselves, we want to spend more time with them. When someone makes us cry and feel inadequate, these negative feelings are a signal that there is something wrong with the relationship. If we are listening to our emotional signals, we start to think we should stay away from that person or change our relationship with them so that we feel better in that relationship. From this point of view, feeling sad when we have lost something important or have been let down is not only normal, it is adaptive.

BLIND SPOTS

Through working with depressed women, I have come to believe that depression develops when the signal functions of emotion are lost. For a reason that makes sense if I'm standing in the client's shoes, feeling depressed is better than admitting a truth about a relationship with someone important that would lead to profound feelings of sadness. One depressed woman, whom you will come to know well in these pages, did not want to admit that her mother had neglected her as a child. It was less painful to blame herself for the ill-treatment she received than to consider the possibility that her mother didn't love her.

These unacknowledged truths are what I think of as *blind spots*. A blind spot is something about an important relationship that we don't want to see.

When we're learning to drive, we're taught to check our blind spots so we don't get any nasty surprises. As we gain experience driving, we develop intuitions about what might be in our blind spots. We might think, "Where's that blue minivan that was beside me at the light?" We sense that there is something there even when we can't see it. Psychological blind spots are the same. Often what is in our blind spot is something that we both know and don't know at the same time. We have an uneasy feeling that something is there, but we can't see what it is unless we look.

As a therapist, it is my job to help a client look at her blind spots. When a depressed woman walks into my office, she is typically struggling to make herself feel better, to pull herself together, to stop feeling bad. She might tell herself she has nothing to complain about, that other people's lives are much worse than hers, or that her family or marriage is not so bad. She sees herself as weak and unable to tolerate normal problems of living. She tries to suppress her unhappiness because she sees that when she puts it into words, her complaints cause conflict. She would like me to join in this effort with her. She would like me to give her strategies to cope with her difficulties and build her self-esteem so she no longer feels the pain and hurt she repeatedly endures. One of the hardest things I have to do at the beginning of therapy is to tell her that I can't help her. I have to tell her that I have never met a depressed person who didn't have something genuinely painful to feel depressed about. I have to tell her that my goal is not to silence her but to help her listen to her emotions to find out what is wrong in her life.

THREE WOMEN

I would like to introduce you to three women I treated for depression in my private practice. I will be telling you their stories in this book, partly to illustrate the theories and research I discuss and partly to show how depressed women can make changes in their lives that make them feel better. All of their stories are true, but their names and other identifying information have been changed to protect their identities. In some cases, I have combined similar stories into one narrative. I will tell you their stories as I learned them myself so that you can see how they gradually saw what was in their blind spots and the hidden relationship patterns that contributed to their depression.

At this point, I would like to tell you what they told me in their first therapy sessions.

Lisa

Lisa was a slim woman with long blonde hair that made her seem much younger than her age. She was soft-spoken and demure. She wore jeans and a T-shirt to our first session and sipped coffee from a take-out cup. She seemed like a gentle, overly polite teenager rather than a thirty-year-old woman with children.

Lisa came to see me at the insistence of a friend she met through playing folk music. Lisa was proud of the beautiful, haunting music she created. She told me that as a young woman she had briefly attended music school but had dropped out to marry her first husband. That marriage ended quickly when she discovered he was "a liar and a cheat." Just before the end of her marriage, she met David, who became her second husband. When she moved out of the home she shared with her first husband, she moved in with David because she had nowhere else to go. Within a year she was pregnant. From that time on she devoted herself to looking after their home and children, who were two and four years old.

Lisa described her marriage as lacking warmth and intimacy from the beginning. David was a pilot and spent months at a time away from home. On the rare occasions he was home, Lisa found him to be emotionally distant, sexually demanding, and physically abusive.

Lisa had known for some time that David had affairs, especially when he traveled for work. The year before I met her, he had had an affair with her younger sister. Lisa came to see me because she had just learned that he had had an affair while away on a work assignment. The affair had resulted in a child whom David wanted to acknowledge and support financially. Lisa usually tolerated his affairs because they reduced his sexual demands on her, but this time she thought he was "asking too much."

Lisa cried throughout our appointment. She said she had been foolish to trust a man who was so obviously unreliable. She believed she had made "dumb choices" about men, and she expressed more anger toward herself for being "stupid" than toward David for betraying her. She blamed herself for their problems. A lot of the conflict between them revolved around sex. Whenever they made love, she felt used by him. She told me he would pester her for days, and when she finally relented, he would "finish quickly" and go sleep in the spare bedroom so he could get a good night's sleep. She felt debased by his treatment, but she did not blame him for making her feel this way because she believed her only value as a woman came from being a "sex object."

Anne

Anne was a tall, striking woman in her fifties. She had stylishly cut gray hair, and she wore expensive clothes. For our initial meeting, she wore a skirt and matching sweater set that she had carefully accessorized with pearls. Despite her attractive appearance, she was not a pleasant woman. Frequently, she seemed annoyed by my questions. The folds of a frown would gather between her eyebrows, and her mouth would turn downward in a sour expression. However, she didn't express irritation with me. Instead, she commented sharply that the doctor who had referred her said I was very competent, so I must know what I was doing.

Anne came to therapy because she was struggling with a recent separation from her husband. She told me that she was not sleeping or eating and that she felt so weighed down she was unable to move. Although she felt lonely and sad about the end of the marriage, she was more aware of her anger toward her husband, Bill. He had ended their marriage suddenly by announcing that he was moving out because he was unable to change his "unacceptable marital behavior." Anne did not want to say what that behavior was. She said that the marriage had been unhappy for many years and that they both would be better off out of it, but she was bitter about the years she had wasted. She also was afraid of what would happen to her in the future. They did not have children, so they were financially comfortable, but she worried she would be left "alone and penniless" in old age.

At first, she declined to discuss her husband or their marriage except to say she married him when she was about thirty because she had been "desperate." She said that talking about the past made her feel sad and wouldn't change anything. With some gentle persistence, she told me that they had moved often because he was in the military, and he expected her to "hit the ground running" in each of their new homes. When she would say she felt lonely or sad about leaving a previous home, he would tell her to get over it. She assumed that his response meant he didn't really care about her. Over time, she withdrew her emotional energy from their marriage and invested it in her work.

Tracy

Tracy had long, curly dark hair. She had gained about thirty pounds during pregnancy and had given up trying to dress attractively. Like many new mothers, she wore sweatpants and a baggy sweatshirt to our first session. She was a lively and cheerful young woman who told her story with a dry eye and an even drier wit.

Tracy was referred to me by her family physician for treatment of postpartum depression. When I first met her, she had been treated for depression for several months. Initially she had responded to antidepressants, but later she slipped into a severe depression. About a month before I met her, she had been admitted to a psychiatric hospital because she had planned to kill herself.

Tracy didn't know she needed professional help until she noticed she was crying all the time. She couldn't explain what triggered these bouts of crying. She only knew she felt completely overwhelmed by looking after her baby. She felt tired all the time and spent hours every day lying in bed, doing nothing. She tried to go back to work because she thought that might help her feel better, but she was unable to cope and returned home after only a few weeks. She was only able to do one thing in a day, such as grocery shopping or laundry. Often she found herself standing in a store staring at the shelves, unable to choose between products, and when she looked at her watch she would see that a couple of hours had passed since she'd entered the store.

Tracy had had periods of feeling low as an adolescent, but she had never experienced a full-blown episode of depression until after her son's birth. She said she wasn't the kind of person to get depressed. She was used to being busy and responsible. She had always coped with whatever life threw at her and usually had had enough energy left over to support her sister and mother too. Her parents had divorced when Tracy was a little girl, and she had helped her mother by looking after her younger sister. Later she put herself through university.

Tracy and her partner Matt had lived together for several years before having a child. She described their relationship as fun and companionable. During her pregnancy, they were both excited and happy. However, after their son was born, Matt "checked out" by working long hours, being distant, and refusing to help with the baby. After Tracy was hospitalized for depression, Matt seemed to turn back into an affectionate and supportive partner, but now she worried that he would "bail" on her again at some time in the future. She said he had never been very interested in her sexually, and since having the baby, he rarely wanted sex. She felt he avoided her by working long hours and spending evenings on the telephone with customers. By the time he was ready for bed she was usually asleep. He would sleep in the spare bedroom, saying that he didn't want to disturb her or be disturbed when she got up with the baby during the night. Although he was affectionate, she worried that he didn't really love her and that he regretted having a baby with her.

Different but the Same

Lisa, Anne, and Tracy are very different women. They were all severely depressed, but their depression was expressed in different ways. Of the three women, only Lisa seemed classically depressed. She cried and blamed herself for her husband's infidelity; crying and self-blame are the hallmarks of depression. Her depression was apparent enough that her friend recognized it and suggested she seek help.

The other two women were referred by their family physicians. They were lucky to have their depression recognized by physicians. Family physicians misdiagnose two-thirds of the depressed people who come to see them (Coyne, Schwenk, and Fechner-Bates 1995), wrongly giving them ineffective treatments like sleeping pills. Like many people who seek treatment from their family doctor, Anne's depression was expressed primarily in physical symptoms. She was not especially aware of feeling sad; her predominant feelings were anger and regret. Although we usually think of depressed people as sad, in fact, many are irritable and angry, at least on the surface.

Of the three women, Tracy appeared the least depressed to an outsider. Although she cried constantly when she was alone, she was unable to connect her crying to a feeling. Like Anne, her depression was expressed primarily in physical symptoms. Unlike Anne, her cheerful personality allowed her to put on a happy face that made her seem fine to her family and friends.

Despite these differences, the three women's stories have similarities. All three had problems in their romantic relationships. As I discuss in chapter 8, relationship distress is strongly connected to depression. In my clinical experience, very few depressed people are satisfied with their intimate relationships, even if this was not the original cause of their depression. Interestingly, all three women saw their partners as detached and indifferent to them. Depressed people are likely to see their partners this way, and their partners are likely to behave in ways that convey detachment (Whiffen 2005). Believing that your partner does not care about you is highly likely to make you feel depressed. As we will see in chapter 8, however, not all detached partners are indifferent.

Finally, in all three stories we see the seeds of the problems that brought these women into therapy. Lisa tolerated her husband's affairs to avoid dealing with what she experienced as his sexual abusiveness; Anne married a man because she was desperate; Tracy had a baby with a buddy who showed little sexual interest in her. In the end, Lisa's husband brought his affair into their home; Anne's husband left her after a long, loveless marriage; Tracy's buddy found her unattractive when she had a baby. In retrospect, these outcomes seem almost inevitable, yet why would Lisa, Anne, and Tracy deliberately choose paths that would end so painfully for them? The answer is that they wouldn't. These seeds gave me my first hints of what was in their blind spots.

Questions to Ask Yourself

1. How many times have I been depressed? When was my first episode? When was my worst episode? Is depression a revolving door for me?

2. How many of the symptoms of depression do I have right now? Should I think about seeing a physician or a mental health professional about these symptoms?

CHAPTER 2

body & mind

Don't skip this chapter! Most people who are interested in psychology glaze over when I start talking about the biological processes involved in depression. These processes can be hard to understand, but I've done the difficult part by wading through dozens of research papers on hormones, genetics, and the neurochemistry of stress. What you'll find in this chapter is a plain-language explanation of these topics so that you will know some of the biological reasons you might experience depression.

Both life experiences and biological factors contribute to depression. For most of this book, I talk about women's experiences, but in this chapter I discuss three aspects of biology that have been researched in the context of depression: hormones, genetics, and how our bodies react to stress. As I will describe, the research shows that although girls and women are more likely to become depressed when they go through puberty or have a baby, there is no evidence that depression at these times is caused by reproductive hormones. We do know that depression runs in families and that a woman's risk is greater if her parents, aunts and uncles, or grandparents suffered from depression. However, genetic risk is only part of the story. Whether a woman with the genetic risk experiences depression depends a great deal on what happens to her during her life. Almost everyone who becomes depressed does so after experiencing a severe life stressor. Women with the genetic risk for depression may react strongly to stress at a biological level, and this reaction may play a part in why they become depressed.

RAGING HORMONES

Girls' and women's rates of depression are highest during their reproductive years, between puberty and menopause. Puberty occurs between the ages of ten and fourteen, when girls develop breasts, grow body hair, and begin to menstruate. Puberty increases a girl's risk for depression, regardless of the age at which these changes occur (Angold, Costello, and Worthman 1998). In addition, depression rates go up significantly when women have babies. Between 10 and 15 percent of women develop depression either during pregnancy or in the postpartum period; this rate is more than double the average rate for women of childbearing age (Whiffen 1992).

These facts have led many people to believe that women's depression is due to hormones. They mean *reproductive hormones*, like estrogen and progesterone, which govern our reproductive cycles. The levels of these hormones go up and down, often dramatically, as we menstruate and have babies. This hormonal activity is thought to cause mood swings. In short, raging hormones are thought to make us depressed.

The power of this belief is enormous. It is so great that you may not believe me when I say that there is no evidence that reproductive hormones cause depression. Researchers have looked at how much estrogen and progesterone we have in our bodies, the ratio of one to the other, and how quickly one or the other either drops or climbs when we go through something like childbirth. They have found no link with depression. Hormones do not directly cause us to become depressed (Young and Korszun 1998).

A small number of researchers are now talking about an indirect link. We know that reproductive hormones change the way *neurotransmitters* are made and used by the nervous system. Neurotransmitters are chemicals in the brain and nervous system that influence our moods, including feelings of depression. We know that reproductive hormones have an impact on *serotonin*, a neurotransmitter that is highly involved in depression. However, at this time, it is not clear how this might lead to depression.

What About PMS?

Maybe you're confused. Maybe you're one of the 80 percent of women who experience *premenstrual syndrome* (PMS) and feel irritable, depressed, or moody just before their period. You might even be one of the 5 to 10 percent for whom symptoms are so severe that they've sought treatment. Your personal experience is that hormones affect how you feel. You will probably be surprised to learn that there is no clear hormonal reason why women experience the mood symptoms of PMS. Any way that researchers have thought to look at it, the hormonal functioning of women with PMS is no different from that of women who do not experience PMS.

However, there are many ways in which women with PMS are similar to women with depression (Landen and Eriksson 2003). About half of the women who suffer from PMS also have episodes of depression. PMS and depression share the same risk factors, including life stress. The most effective medical treatment for PMS is the same class of antidepressants that is used to treat depression—selective serotonin reuptake inhibitors (SSRIs), such as Prozac (fluoxetine). As a result, many researchers have concluded that PMS is a form of depression. Alternatively, both PMS and depression could be due to the same underlying biological process, such as a problem with the way serotonin is made and used by the nervous system.

What About Postpartum Depression?

Isn't that due to hormones?

Almost every article that is published in the popular press says so, but no, *postpartum depression* (PPD) is not caused by reproductive hormones. Again, no study has shown that the hormones of women with PPD are any different from those of new mothers who are not depressed.

A small subgroup of women seems to become depressed only after childbirth, not at other times in their lives (Cooper and Murray 1995). These women have their first episode of depression after giving birth, and about 40 percent of them go on to experience another episode of PPD. Having had severe PMS may be a risk factor for being in this subgroup. However, researchers have not looked to see if being in this subgroup is related to a hormonal problem.

The only hormones involved in the development of PPD are those associated with the thyroid. In a small number of cases, childbirth triggers thyroid problems and depression (Harris et al. 1989). Often this depression can be treated by treating the thyroid problem, but this is not always the case. Tracy was diagnosed with thyroid problems that were subsequently treated, but the treatment did not help her depression.

Most of the women who experience PPD have either been depressed before or they go on to experience another depression that is not related to having a baby. These women are at risk for depression throughout their lives.

As is true with PMS, the risk factors for PPD are the same as those for depression generally (Whiffen 1992). Some women become depressed when they experience significant life stress that may or may not have anything to do with a baby. Other episodes are related to marital problems and to lack of support from the husband or romantic partner. Relationship factors are particularly important when women have a history of depression. One study examined a group of pregnant women who had been depressed previously. Those who became depressed again after childbirth were in relationships with men who seemed indifferent to them (Marks et al. 1996).

What About Menopause?

Menopause starts when a woman has gone for twelve months without having a period. The time that leads up to menopause is called *perimenopause* or the *transition to menopause*. This period can last for up to five years. During this time, women's hormones are fluctuating while their overall estrogen levels are declining. Their menstrual cycles are variable in length and flow, and they skip some periods. They experience classic symptoms like hot flashes and night sweats as well as moodiness. If hormones are involved in women's depression, then the hormonal roller-coaster ride that leads up to menopause should put women at risk.

Nancy Avis (2003) reviewed the research on depression during menopause. She found no evidence that menopause increases women's risk for depression. The overall rate of depression does not go up when women go through menopause. In addition, hormones are not connected to whether or not a woman experiences depression at this time in her life.

Who are the women that become depressed during perimenopause? Women may be at risk if perimenopause lasts more than two years. Over a long period of time, symptoms like hot flashes and night sweats disrupt women's sleep and wear them down emotionally. Women who have a history of PMS or PPD also are at risk for depression during perimenopause. These women may be part of that subgroup that seems susceptible to depression during periods of hormonal change, although again, there is no evidence that hormones themselves cause these women to become depressed.

Life stress is the biggest factor that puts perimenopausal women at risk. There is a lot going on in women's lives at this age. They may be caring for ill parents or grieving a parent's death. They may have serious health concerns of their own. They may experience other kinds of stress that any of us could, like financial or work problems. The kinds of life events that trigger depression in perimenopausal women are the same as those that trigger depression at other times in women's lives.

Puberty and Childbirth: Big Changes for Girls and Women

There are only two times during which our hormones are raging that we are also at greater risk than usual for depression: puberty and childbirth. But as we have seen, there is no direct connection between how crazy our hormones get and whether we become depressed. So what other factors might cause an increase in depression at these times?

Both puberty and childbirth are big events in girls' and women's lives. Pubertal girls are becoming women. Their bodies are changing. They are discovering sex. They are maturing both emotionally and cognitively. The adolescent brain is going through as much growth and development as the brain of a toddler. That's a lot for a fourteen-year-old girl to handle. Pregnant women are becoming mothers. Their bodies are changing too! They are discovering the lifelong challenges and rewards of motherhood. Their lives will never be the same. Many researchers believe that girls and women are at risk for depression during puberty and childbearing periods because of the many social and emotional changes that they face at these times.

DEPRESSION RUNS IN FAMILIES

Genetics is the study of how biological characteristics are passed on from parents to children. Sullivan, Neale, and Kendler (2000) reviewed the research linking depression to genetic factors. In contrast to the findings for reproductive hormones, they found that genes clearly play a part in depression.

Researchers can do different kinds of studies to see whether genes are involved in medical and psychiatric disorders. One type of study involves starting with a group of people with depression and seeing if depression is more common among their relatives than it is in the general population. If genes play a part, the researcher expects to see higher rates of depression among family members. The highest rates are expected among the parents, siblings, and children of depressed people because these relatives have the most genes in common.

Studies of this type show that depression, particularly recurrent depression, runs in families. If you have a history of depression, your relatives are at three times the normal risk. Conversely, if one of your parents or siblings has a history of depression, you are at increased risk too.

A second type of study involves twins. Identical twins have all the same genes. If depression is influenced by genes, then you would expect identical twins to have a similar history of depression. When the twin method is used, it is again clear that genes play a part.

However, if you think of the causes of depression as a pie, genetics account for only about one-third of the pie. The remaining two-thirds is due to what scientists call *nonshared environmental influences*. These are things that happen to one identical twin but not the other. These events explain more about depression than do the genes the twins have in common.

Some of these nonshared events happened in the past. For instance, one twin could have been sexually abused as a child while the other twin was not. Nonshared environmental factors that happened in the past account for another third in the depression pie. Finally, some nonshared events happen just before the depressive episode begins and account for the final third of the depression pie. Specific episodes of depression are almost always preceded by a severely stressful life event or a severe, persistent problem (Kessler 1997). For most people, the genetic risk must be activated by a severe life stressor. For instance, one twin could go through a marital separation while the other twin does not.

Depression is not like your mother's blue eyes or your aunt's red hair. No single gene is responsible for depression. A number of genes are involved, none of which has been identified so far. This means that one woman may have a lot of the genes that are involved while another may have only a few of them. The woman with more genes will be at greater risk. If you have relatives on both sides of your family who have experienced depression, you may be at greater genetic risk because you may have inherited some of the genes from both sides.

Depression does run in families, and the genetic influences on depression are substantial. However, that is only part of the story. Whether a woman with the genetic risk becomes depressed depends on what happens to her. Genetic risk and life stress must come together to produce depression.

The Genetic Risk

What exactly is being inherited when we say that someone has the genetic risk? There are a lot of possibilities because there are many biological differences between people who experience depression and those who do not. People with depression differ from nondepressed persons in the levels of neurotransmitters in their brains, particularly of serotonin. Some parts of their brains also are more developed and active, and they differ in their sleep and dreaming patterns. At this time, we do not know if these biological differences actually cause depression or if they are the result of another underlying biological process.

STRESS REACTIVITY

One possibility is the way our bodies respond to stress. As I mentioned earlier, people with the genetic risk do not usually become depressed unless they experience severe life stressors. About half of the people who experience depression react strongly to even mild levels of stress, and they take longer than usual to calm down (Southwick, Vythilingam, and Charney 2005). It is possible that what we inherit with the genetic risk for depression is a biological tendency to react strongly to stress.

There are two kinds of stress: acute and chronic. An *acute stressor* is one that happens suddenly and is over with quickly. You experience an *acute stress response* when you are in sudden danger. When stress is *chronic*, the stress keeps coming instead of being resolved. A *chronic stressor* is a problem that doesn't change much over the short term, like not making enough money to support yourself and your family.

The human stress response system is geared toward handling acute stressors. For example, when you are driving and another car swerves into your lane, you experience an acute stress response. Your heart beats quickly, and you suddenly feel afraid. The purpose of this response is to get you to react quickly so that you can get out of the way of the other car. For a couple of minutes after you've avoided the accident, you may feel keyed up, and it may take awhile for your heartbeat and breathing to return to normal, but within a few minutes you calm down.

When we experience acute stress, our bodies mobilize for action. The *hypothalamic-pituitary-adrenal (HPA) axis* is a hormonal pathway that turns on to help us to cope with the stressor, either by running away from it or by fighting back. Symptoms that show the HPA axis has been switched on include feelings of fear or anxiety, physical restlessness, not being able to focus attention, not feeling hungry, and having trouble sleeping, especially having trouble getting to sleep or waking up earlier than usual. As I described in chapter 1, these are also symptoms of depression (except for the feelings of fear or anxiety).

Cortisol is the hormone most closely associated with stress. Normally, as soon as the amount of cortisol in your body gets to a certain level, another system kicks in to shut down the stress response. However, the shutdown system doesn't always work properly. It could be that you have inherited a shutdown system that takes longer to engage. You may always have been the kind of person who takes a long time to get over being upset. If the shutdown system doesn't work properly, our bodies keep releasing cortisol. After a few days of having a lot of cortisol in our system, we begin to feel tired, helpless, and depressed.

What Determines How Reactive We Are?

Some people are born with a tendency to react strongly to stress. Even as babies they are easily upset and hard to soothe. Other people have learned to react strongly to stress. In childhood, they were exposed to high levels of uncontrollable stress (Southwick, Vythilingam, and Charney 2005). They may have been physically or sexually abused or left alone for long periods of time. They may have been repeatedly bullied at school or picked on by teachers. When children experience severe, uncontrollable stress, they can react strongly to stress for years afterward.

As Southwick and colleagues (2005) describe, experiences early in our lives can program the way we react to stress. Rat pups that are separated from their mothers or whose mothers are stressed are strongly responsive to stress later in their lives. In contrast, rat pups that are stroked and groomed every day, even by a human, are resilient to stress. This is exactly what we see with people. People who experienced abuse as children are highly reactive to stress and have great difficulty calming down. Their stress shutdown system is damaged and takes a long time to kick in. In contrast, people who experienced warm, caring relationships with their parents are able to cope with a wide variety of stressful experiences.

Whether stress reactivity is inherited through our genes or learned through life experience, researchers now believe it is a piece of the puzzle in explaining depression.

Chronic Stress

Women are at risk for depression following either a severely stressful life event or a severe, chronic stressor. Certain kinds of chronic stressors are more likely than others to result in depression (Anisman and Matheson 2005). The kind of stress that leads to depression is one that *varies in intensity*. The situation could be bad for a few days, then improve, then get much worse again. These periods of improvement and worsening are *unpredictable*. A woman never knows when she wakes up in the morning how stressful her day is going to be.

When stress is chronic but unpredictable as well as variable in intensity, the stress response system has no chance to shut down. Whenever it begins to shut down, something new happens to trigger another stress response. When it does not shut down, our bodies continue to produce cortisol, with the resulting depression-like symptoms that I described above.

Conflict in an important relationship is a good example of this kind of stress. The relationship could be with anyone: a close friend, a boss or coworker, a parent, or a romantic partner or spouse. The important factor is that the woman must interact frequently with this person.

A conflicted relationship can be stable; over time it may not get much better or worse. We can adapt to a bad relationship that is always the same. It may not make us happy, but at least it is predictable. However, most bad relationships cause conflict. Conflict is upsetting and seems to come out of nowhere for the people involved. So for most people, relationship conflict is a chronic stressor that occasionally and unpredictably gets worse. Our bodies cannot adapt to this kind of stress because we are constantly mobilized by conflict.

Many episodes of depression seem to result from the combination of chronic, unpredictable stress and a stress response system that is highly activated and doesn't shut down. This may be one of the reasons depression is strongly linked to being unhappily married.

Women and Stress

One reason researchers are so interested in stress reactivity is that women have a stronger biological reaction to stressful life events than men do (Anisman and Matheson 2005). Women also experience more of the kind of stress that is likely to lead to depression, particularly interpersonal and chronic stress (Tennant 2002). So stress reactivity could explain why women are at greater risk for depression than men.

BODY AND MIND

Our bodies and minds are linked. What is happening in our bodies affects our moods, including feelings of depression. At this time, reproductive hormones do not appear to play a direct part in women's depression. However, genetic factors do. Depression runs in families. What we may inherit when we inherit the genetic risk is not a specific gene for depression. However, we may inherit a tendency to react strongly to stress and/or to have difficulty shutting down our stress response. Stress reactivity also can be learned if a child experiences severe stress over which she has little control. Specific episodes of depression are triggered by severe life stress or chronic, unpredictable stressors that periodically get worse. The combination of life stress and a stress response system that is hyperreactive may result in depression for many women.

Questions to Ask Yourself

1. How many of my relatives have experienced depression? (Don't forget to count both sides of your family.)

2. Do I get more stressed than other people I know? Do I get upset about little things that don't bother others? Does it take me longer to calm down when I get upset?

3. When I was a kid, did something happen to me that was really stressful and felt totally out of my control? Was I abused or bullied?

4. Is there a situation in my life now that is chronically stressful for me? Do I have conflict with someone I have to deal with all the time?

CHAPTER 3

the process of living is stressful

In the early years of stress research, a physician named Stanley Sarnoff observed that stress is a normal part of life. As he put it, "The process of living is the process of having stress imposed on you and reacting to it" (Sarnoff 1963, 100). Yet almost every episode of depression is triggered by either a stressful life event or a period of chronic stress. If stress is normal, why doesn't everyone become depressed?

BIG, BAD EVENTS

Specific kinds of stress usually happen right before a woman becomes depressed (Kessler 1997). Generally speaking, the stress that triggers depression is severe, and the impact on the woman is significant.

Something serious happens that makes her feel devalued or diminished. To trigger depression, stress must be big and it must be bad.

Losses

Losses occur when someone important to us leaves our life, for instance because the relationship is over or because they die. Often this person has been a *confidante*, someone you could turn to for emotional support when you were stressed or felt upset. We also suffer losses when we lose our jobs or experience failure in an important area of life, like school, work, marriage, or motherhood. Losses often lead to depression. If a woman is going to become depressed after a loss, this usually happens right away, within the first month or so after the loss occurs (Tennant 2002).

If a single loss is big enough and bad enough, it can trigger depression. For example, Lisa learned that her husband David had fathered a child by a woman he met while working away from home. This revelation was a loss for Lisa. Although David had had affairs before, he had never become seriously attached to another woman. Lisa lost her conviction that no matter how many women David had sex with, he would always be her husband. She felt devalued by his betrayal, both as his wife and as the mother of his children. She became depressed almost immediately.

Women also can become depressed when they experience several losses over a short period of time. The year before Anne became depressed, her husband Bill was transferred in his job. Anne left behind many friends as well as a job she loved in the city she considered her home. She was trying to come to terms with these losses when, a few months later, Bill told her he was leaving her. Soon after, she became depressed. Anne had been unhappily married for many years, and she thought she and Bill would be happier apart. She felt devalued by Bill's rejection, but she might have been able to cope with the end of their marriage if she had not already suffered several other losses.

Chronic Stress

Chronic stress also is a source of depression. For women, interpersonal stressors (such as marital conflict, troubled relationships with close friends or family members, or ongoing conflict with a boss or coworker) are the most depressing. Chronic stressors usually are less intense than losses, especially when they first develop, so there is more of a lag between when the stress starts and when a woman becomes depressed. Stress of this kind can lead to depression after about six months (Tennant 2002). However, chronic stress is more likely than a single loss to result in a long period of depression. If the situation does not improve, a woman may get caught in a revolving door. She may experience separate episodes of depression as the problem gets better and worse.

Chronic stress can make a loss worse. Clinicians who work with depressed women often see this pattern. A woman struggles with a chronic stressor. Eventually, the situation deteriorates to the point that she experiences a loss. Then she becomes depressed.

A client named Suzanne was unhappily married for many years. Her children picked up on their parents' conflict. One was anxious and refused to go to school; another was aggressive with teachers and other kids. Suzanne and her husband disagreed about how to handle the children's problems, which added to their marital conflict. The situation spiraled downward until eventually their oldest son left home after a fight with his father. At this point, Suzanne became depressed. Although her depression immediately followed her son leaving home, this loss might not have triggered depression under different circumstances. Suzanne's marital problems and the difficulties with her children led her to question herself as a wife and mother. When her son left home, she was convinced she had failed.

Transitions

Whenever we leave one role to take on a new one, we are making a *transition*. Major life transitions used to be rare: people left school to start work; they got married, had kids, and retired. People's lives change a great deal more now than they once did. Every time we change jobs, move homes, or end a romantic relationship, we create a transition. Transitions create stress, and this stress can lead to depression.

Sometimes it's hard for a woman to see a connection between a transition and her depression. Change in life is often a good thing.

Perhaps we are moving on to a new phase of life or finally achieving something we have longed for. The positive side of the transition can make it hard to see the downside. But no matter how good we feel about the change, transitions are stressful.

Some are stressful because they make us feel anxious and unsure of ourselves. These transitions challenge us to prove ourselves in new ways. For instance, when women first become mothers, they often have had little previous experience with babies. They may not know much about feeding or soothing them or getting them to sleep. More important, they may question their ability to be good mothers. They may worry about providing the right kind of environment and making the right choices. When we don't know how well we're doing in a new role, we feel stressed. Starting a new job or course at school can be stressful for the same reason.

It is also very difficult to make a transition without losing something we value. Often we don't know how much we value a part of our life until it is gone. For instance, one woman became depressed when she moved across the country to take her dream job. She hadn't expected to miss her friends, family, boyfriend, and even her hometown.

Transitions often result in our losing contact with people who are important to us. When we move, we lose daily contact with familiar people. We may leave behind family or close friends whom we used to see regularly. When we have lived somewhere for a long time, we can take this contact for granted. No matter how much we look forward to the move and how much better we expect our lives to be in our new home, when we make the move, we suddenly become aware of what we have lost.

When we are stressed, we turn to the people who are close to us for comfort and support. However, transitions can make those people unavailable to us. Sometimes we lose contact with them as part of the transition. When Anne and Bill first separated, she used to ask for his advice as she had done throughout their marriage. However, he made it clear he no longer wanted to help with her problems.

Sometimes people are unavailable because they are going through the transition too. Couples who have just had a baby are a good example. Having a baby, especially the first one, is stressful for both men and women, although in different ways. Couples have to make a transition from being romantic partners to parents and from being the children of their parents to parents themselves. Women are concerned with how well they are doing as mothers. They need to hear they're doing a good job and that their husbands value their work as mothers. Men are concerned about being left behind. Many men feel excluded by the close bond that develops between a new mother and her baby. They need to hear they are still important.

Sometimes new parents are so busy coping with their own stress they don't realize how stressful the transition is for their partner. This was true for Matt and Tracy. Matt had always been Tracy's best friend. When their son was born, she expected him to pitch in with the housework so that she could focus on taking care of their baby. When he didn't, she felt devalued. She felt Matt didn't care about her and their baby and that he didn't value her work as a mother. This wasn't true. As we will see in chapter 8, Matt admired Tracy's abilities as a mother. In fact, he thought she was such a good mother that he was irrelevant. He was too caught up in his own feelings to see that she needed him to support her as he had done in the past.

WHY ME?

Couples break up all the time. Our parents die. Our children worry us. We are unhappy at work or have financial problems. We lose our jobs or fail to reach our goals. Our lives change, for better and for worse. As Sarnoff said, the process of living is stressful. Yet only a fraction of the people who experience stress become depressed. Why are some people at more risk than others?

Women with a family history of depression are three times more likely than other women to get depressed when they experience significant stress (Kessler 1997). As I discussed in chapter 2, stress may trigger a strong biological reaction in these women that doesn't shut down when it should.

Women also are at risk when they are struggling to cope with more than one stressor at a time. Most women who experience three or more significant stressors within a year become depressed (Monroe and Simons 1991). While Anne might have been able to cope with one or two losses, she wasn't able to cope with all of them happening at once.

Women are more susceptible to stress when they've been depressed before (Kessler 1997). It takes a severe stressor to provoke depression in a woman who has never been depressed. But after the first time, she is at risk when she experiences stress that is not as severe. Women who have had several episodes can become depressed again when they experience life events that some of us would not consider stressful.

Each episode of depression may make a woman's body more reactive to stress. Another possibility is that depression leaves scars that influence the way we cope with stress. After women recover from depression, they lack confidence in themselves and are more withdrawn than they were before becoming depressed (Coyne and Calarco 1995). They may be less willing to open up and take risks in their relationships. Interpersonal sensitivity and mistrust may get in the way of resolving interpersonal problems when they arise.

Women who have a history of depression are at *forty times* the usual risk for another episode when they experience life stress (Kessler 1997).

A VICIOUS CYCLE

Once a woman becomes depressed, she is likely to behave in ways that create more stress, particularly of the interpersonal kind (Hammen 2003). Because stress is both a cause of depression and one of its consequences, women can get caught in a vicious cycle.

There are at least three reasons why depression makes stress worse. First, as I discuss in chapters 8 and 9, depression has a negative impact on the relationships women have with their romantic partners and children. Family members are quick to get angry with each other, and there is more conflict in the home.

Second, depression interferes with our ability to solve problems. Our negative mood colors the way we look at problems and makes us pessimistic about solving them. Often we feel so helpless that we don't even try. We have difficulty staying focused when we are thinking about problems, and it is hard to make decisions. The symptoms of depression work against coping well with stress.

Third, as I discussed in chapter 2, our stress response system is activated when we are depressed. Once it is turned on, our bodies react strongly even to mild levels of stress. A minor disagreement can balloon into a major conflict because we lack the patience and tolerance needed to get along with others. A small problem becomes a catastrophe.

When Bill left Anne, she had to find a job to support herself, so she accepted a short-term clerical position. She got along well with the other employees, but from the start, she had problems with the boss. He never praised Anne for doing her job well; he only spoke to her when she had done something wrong. He also made decisions without consulting his employees, which made Anne angry. He reminded her of Bill, who was critical of her and always made the decisions in their marriage without asking what she thought. I agreed with her that he sounded like a difficult boss. However, I noticed that Anne was the only employee who got into frequent conflicts with him. When her contract ended, he decided to let her go.

Anne's conflict with her boss was one of the factors that kept her depressed. She believed that her inability to solve her problems with him stemmed from the same deficiency that stopped her from solving her problems with Bill. She concluded that she was a failure at getting men to respond to her needs. When Anne lost her job, her depression became much worse.

WAYS OF COPING

When we are stressed, we try to cope. There are almost as many ways of coping as there are people who cope, but research psychologists usually divide coping into two broad types. The first coping strategy is aimed at *solving the problem*. We can try to solve a problem by thinking about the stressful situation and experimenting with ways to improve it. We also can try to solve a problem by turning to other people for help and support. Talking to others calms us down and may give us new ways of thinking about the problem. Problem solving is a good coping strategy that works well in a wide variety of situations. Generally speaking, problem solvers are less likely to become depressed.

The second strategy is to *avoid or ignore the problem.* Such coping strategies are less effective than problem solving and are often associated with depression. We can avoid our problems by drinking alcohol, using drugs, overeating, gambling, shopping compulsively, watching TV, playing video games, or fantasizing about winning the lottery. These coping strategies may make us feel better for a while, but in the long run the situation doesn't improve, so we continue to be stressed.

Loss of Control

These different ways of coping are linked to how much control we think we have over a problem (Anisman and Matheson 2005). Obviously, there are some stressful situations in which we are genuinely powerless. A child who is being abused by her parent really has no control. No matter what she does or doesn't do, the abuse will continue as long as the parent chooses to abuse her. However, in most of the stressful situations we run into as adults, we have at least some control.

People who believe they are powerless cope by avoiding or ignoring their problems. That makes sense. If nothing we do makes a difference, why bother? We might as well put our coping efforts into feeling better, at least for a little while. Activities like drinking, taking drugs, or watching TV distract us temporarily from painful feelings. However, ignoring problems becomes a self-fulfilling prophesy. If we do nothing, nothing changes. Our feeling of powerlessness is confirmed. In contrast, if we believe we have at least some control, we are more likely to actively search for a solution. While we are trying out different ideas, we will probably try something that works. Having an impact confirms our feeling that we have control.

We are less likely to feel depressed if we believe we have at least some control. One way we can fight depression is by taking control of a stressful situation. However, it is not always easy to see how to do this. From Anne's point of view, Bill had complete control over her life. What Anne wanted didn't seem to matter. What could she have done to take back control? She could have gone back to her hometown when her marriage ended. However, like many depressed women,

Anne did not believe she had control over the stress in her life. Instead of going home, she found a job in the new city. Why would Anne do this? There is usually a good reason why depressed women feel powerless. When you know more about Anne's story, you may understand why she felt she had so little control over her life.

Getting By with a Little Help from Our Friends

One of the most powerful ways we cope is by turning to people we trust for help and emotional support. We don't have to have a lot of friends. What is important is that we are satisfied with the friends we have. We need at least one person we can count on. We can talk openly with this person, and we trust them to understand our point of view. That doesn't mean they always agree with us. Seeing it from our perspective means they understand why we feel as we do, regardless of the way they feel. We also trust this person to have our best interests at heart. Whatever advice this person gives us, we trust they want to help us. This person could be anyone: a friend, a relative, a parent, or a spouse or romantic partner. This person is a *confidante*.

Women are reasonably good at getting by without confidantes as long as their lives are going well, but when they are stressed, the quality of these relationships becomes crucial. If a woman has just one person she can count on, she is protected from depression when she experiences significant life stress (Brown and Harris 1978). Having a supportive spouse or romantic partner is vital, particularly for women (Wade and Kendler 2000). Parents and other relatives are the next most important source of support, especially if a woman lives close to her family and sees them often. Romantic partners and relatives usually have deeper feelings of care for us and a greater sense of commitment to us than do other people.

This may explain why interpersonal stress is so difficult for women. Conflict and tension in relationships is not only stressful; it deprives us of an important source of support.

WHY IS A CONFIDANTE IMPORTANT?

I think everyone needs to feel that their troubles are significant to another person. It's comforting to share them. Sharing makes us feel we are not alone and that someone cares what happens to us. A sense of belonging is an antidote to depression.

Good confidantes also offer good advice. When something big and bad happens, it is normal for people to question themselves. Confidantes can help us think about how a stressful situation developed, what the event means about us, and what consequences it has for our future. They can help us answer these questions in ways that prevent us from becoming depressed (Dobkin et al. 2004).

Every woman has had the experience of comforting a girlfriend who was rejected by a lover or of seeking that comfort herself. A woman who has been rejected wants to understand why. Is there something wrong with her? Will she be rejected by everyone she loves? A confidante can help answer these questions in ways that don't make her feel bad. Instead of concluding that she was rejected because she is unattractive or uninteresting or because she has a fatal flaw in her personality, a confidante can help her form a realistic but nonblaming picture of what happened, what she brought to the situation, and what she can do differently next time. Without someone to talk to, it is difficult to see the stressful situation from a different point of view.

Women without confidantes also may be more likely to avoid or ignore their problems, particularly by drinking or using drugs. This coping method is more likely to lead to depression than to the resolution of a stressful situation.

ANNE: *NO ONE TO TURN TO*

Anne had a lot of friends in the city she thought of as home. She also lived near her sister with whom she had been close all her life. Although she didn't have an emotionally intimate relationship with Bill, she was able to turn to him for help with practical problems. Between her friends, her sister, and Bill, Anne felt supported. When she moved, she lost daily contact with her friends, and her sister now lived a three-hour drive away. Anne started to feel down. So she turned to the last person available to her: Bill.

However, Bill was not very supportive of Anne. Like many depressed women, Anne had married a man who was cold and critical of her. He didn't like Anne when she felt down and helpless, and he had little sympathy for her situation. He told her she was "dependent" and "needy" because she couldn't handle the moves associated with his job. Because he was her only source of feedback, she believed what he said. This made her feel worse. He told her to get on with her life. She tried, but she wasn't enthusiastic about starting over again. Bill was angry with what he saw as her halfhearted attempts to find work and make friends. They fought. The more she turned to him for comfort and support, the more distant Bill became. Then, a few months after they moved, he told her he was leaving.

Bill may have supported Anne in some ways, but he was not a confidante. He couldn't see events from her point of view. He couldn't empathize with how difficult his constant career moves were for her. His lack of empathy meant he couldn't comfort her when she felt down. It wasn't obvious to Anne that Bill was not her confidante as long as she had other people to turn to. Maybe being able to count on him for practical advice made her feel like he was her confidante. When Anne lost the people she usually counted on, the true nature of her relationship with Bill was revealed.

THE PROCESS OF LIVING

Stress is a normal part of life, but normal stress doesn't lead to depression. The kind of stress that leads to depression is stress that devalues her. Lisa was humiliated as a wife and mother; Anne was rejected by her husband; Suzanne had ample evidence that she had failed as a mother; Tracy was convinced Matt didn't love her. In each case, the stressor was a blow to the woman's self-esteem, and had significant implications for her future. Would any of us become depressed under similar circumstances? I strongly suspect we would. But one of the paradoxes of depression is that these kinds of negative events usually happen with our help. In the chapters that follow, I describe how women unwittingly set themselves up to experience the kinds of big, bad events that lead to depression.

Questions to Ask Yourself

1. What happened to me before I became depressed? Did I experience a loss, a chronic stress, or a transition? Did what happened change my life? Was it a blow to my self-esteem? Why?

2. How did I explain this event to myself? What did I tell myself about what caused the event, what it meant about me as a person, and how it affected my future?

3. Has the stress in my life become even worse since I got depressed? Are my reactions making me more stressed?

4. How do I usually cope with stress? How did I cope with what happened to me before I became depressed? How am I coping with being depressed?

5. Do I really lack control in this situation? How could I take more control?

6. Who are my confidantes? Can I talk to them any time I need to? Can I talk about anything with them? Is my confidante part of the problem that is stressing me?

CHAPTER 4

the lives of girls
& women

Women are at greater risk for depression than men are, yet so far it is not clear that this risk stems from their biology. So what is it about the lives of girls and women that leads to depression?

GENDER ROLES

As women we have certain experiences in common. Most of us marry or live with romantic partners. The overwhelming majority have children. Most of us strive to be close to the people who are important to us: our parents, siblings, spouses, lovers, children, and friends. Most of us feel upset when these relationships go badly. Although individual women's lives are unique, in these broad ways we are the same.

Psychologists and sociologists use the term *gender role* to describe these patterns. This term refers not only to the expectations that society has of males and females but also to the behaviors that are typical of the sexes and to the personality traits we associate with them.

Both men and women have gender roles. Men are expected to be physically strong and to work hard to make money for their families. Women are expected to be nice to other people and good mothers. Although not everyone lives up to these expectations, men and women who don't are seen as unusual. Huge social changes have occurred over the past forty years. Yet the man who gives up paid work to stay at home with his kids or the woman who puts her career ahead of her family are viewed with suspicion. Most people don't think much about the impact of gender roles on what they do. However, gender roles are a powerful determinant of both behavior and personality.

Most important, there is a connection between gender roles and depression. Researchers first noticed the link in the 1970s when they realized that not all women are at the same risk for depression. Married women are at greater risk than unmarried women. They also are at greater risk than their husbands, which is surprising because spouses have similar levels of stress in their lives. Yet marriage seems to protect men from becoming depressed. When we consider all possible combinations of sex, marital status, and having kids, the person who is at the lowest risk is a married man and the person who is at the highest risk is a married woman with young children (Bebbington 1996). The woman at greatest risk is the one who is living her gender role.

PINK AND BLUE BLANKETS

Researchers do not know to what extent gender roles are created by actual biological differences between the sexes and how much is due to what children learn. While no researcher doubts that males and females are different biologically, society in the form of parents, peers, and the media also influences the development of gender roles.

There are several ways we teach our children that gender is important. The first is by rewarding them for behaving in ways that are consistent with their gender. This is noticeable in the way parents encourage children's play. For instance, when a little boy plays with toy trucks, parents tend to get down on the floor with him and participate in his play. However, when he picks up his sister's doll, his play tends to be ignored or he may even be told that only girls play with dolls. The parent's enthusiasm is more rewarding than being ignored or told his play is wrong. Children repeat behavior that has been rewarded. In this way, parents shape their children's play consistent with gender roles.

As children get older, messages about gender go well beyond toys. Parents give their children chores that are consistent with their gender. Girls do laundry and housework, while boys mow the lawn. Sons are encouraged to take math and sciences in high school, while daughters are allowed to drop these courses if they are too difficult. Sons are encouraged to pursue careers in engineering and computing science, while daughters are led toward nursing and teaching, careers they can give up when they have children, then return to once the children are in school.

Another way children learn about gender is by watching. Once children figure out that gender is important, they watch what other people of their sex are doing and imitate it, particularly if they expect to be rewarded. Mom praises an older sister for helping her around the house. Dad thanks an older brother for helping him fix something. The younger child sees that these behaviors are rewarded and imitates them. Based on what children see people doing in their families, they develop strong beliefs about what boys and girls "should" do, which they use to guide their own behavior.

To a child, what people do is much more important than what they say. Some writers of children's books have tried to reverse the stereotypes of the past by putting males and females into situations that are unusual for their gender. When my son was young, one of my friends bought him a book about a mommy bear who fixes the baby bear's broken toys. However, I rely on my husband to fix everything from my computer to a burned-out lightbulb. My son thought this book was a comedy and would laugh out loud whenever I read it to him.

One of the first things children learn about themselves is that they are male or female. Adults start this process in the hospital with the pink and blue blankets in which we wrap newborns and the names we choose for them. The ways we praise them ("That's a good girl!"), how we dress them and cut their hair, and all the subtle and not-so-subtle directions that we provide tell children that gender is important to us. They get the message. Once they begin to label themselves as a girl or boy, they start to gather information about gender, and this knowledge has an impact on their behavior.

GENDER AFFECTS WHAT WE DO

By age three, children prefer toys and games that are considered appropriate for their gender: trucks for boys and dolls for girls. By age five, they have future goals for themselves that are typical for their gender. Boys want to become firemen or policemen, while girls want to be nurses or teachers or stay at home to look after children. By the time a child is seven, he or she has an extensive and complex understanding of gender. Children of both sexes will tell you that boys are better at sports and girls are better at art and that mothers take care of children, while fathers go to work. A girl in her early teens may proudly look after her younger brothers and sisters or show interest in cooking and sewing, while a boy of the same age enjoys playing sports and video games. This process continues throughout childhood and reaches a peak in the highly gendered behavior of adolescents—the teenaged boys who constantly jockey for position; the teenaged girls obsessed with boys, fashion, and makeup.

By the time we are adults, men and women are so different that few people dispute the truth in the popular book title *Men Are from Mars, Women Are from Venus* (Gray 1994). Not only do the sexes live on different planets, but the women's planet symbolizes love while the men's planet connotes war.

GENDER AFFECTS WHO WE ARE

Parents encourage girls to be gentle and loving, to be kind to other people, and to feel empathy for them, and boys to compete with other boys, to be dominant, assertive, independent, and decisive. Research psychologists point out that the personality traits that are encouraged in boys and girls are well suited to the gender roles they will occupy as adults. Boys are likely to spend much of their adult lives in the work world and are encouraged to develop traits that will help them thrive in this context. Girls are likely to spend much of their time caring for children and older relatives and are encouraged to develop personality traits that foster relationships, such as empathy and tenderness.

These personality traits are shaped in the same way that girls learn to play with dolls and boys with toy trucks. Parents, teachers, and friends reward girls for being kind and boys for being tough. Once children learn the rules, they make sure they behave in ways that are rewarded. Our teaching is effective. Research that compares males and females shows that girls and women are more empathic and kind than boys and men (Feingold 1994). Girls are more in step with the behavior of other people and better judges of what others are feeling. They are more agreeable and cooperative. They express less anger. Being good at relationships is a source of pride for girls. The better our relationships work, the better we feel about ourselves.

THE DOUBLE SHIFT

Women meet the needs of others. We cook food and clean houses, buy and wash clothes, feed and clean small children, and care for elderly relatives. We also provide emotional care by showing interest in others and by providing comfort and support. In many big and small ways, women show others that they are cared for, and in doing so, we make them feel important and loved.

Work outside the home is also an important part of women's lives in the modern world. Yet the work that must be done to keep families fed, clothed, clean, and cared for remains the responsibility of women (Gjerdingen et al. 2000). The specific activities may have changed, but women spend as much time doing housework and child care as their great-grandmothers did a hundred years ago. The amount of home care that modern husbands do varies a lot from one man to another. However, a significant proportion of men—about a quarter—do almost no housework or child care at all. Many more only do work that is related to their gender role, like gardening and house maintenance. Unlike men, working women can end up doing a *double shift* in which they do both their paid work and their unpaid work in their homes.

For many couples, the greatest imbalance is in the amount of time that men and women spend taking care of their children. Women do twice as much child care as their husbands. In addition, men and women are responsible for different parts of child care. Women look after their children's needs. They provide emotional support and comfort, and they are responsible for scheduling children's activities. Men spend time playing with their children and teaching them skills like riding a bike. Men are least likely to provide care for babies and preschool-aged children because what these children need—physical care—is not part of what a father is expected to provide.

Dads may be fun, but their status as parents is not equal to that of moms. How often have you heard a woman say that her husband is "babysitting" the kids?

The flip side of responsibility is blame. When things go wrong with children—when they are sick or struggling, do badly at school, or have few friends—we are much quicker to blame mothers than fathers, and mothers are much quicker to blame themselves.

AN UNENDING TASK

The female gender role is so demanding that women may feel they can never do a good enough job. For most women, nothing would feel worse than being a bad mother. However, our expectations of mothers are unrealistic. We are supposed to be patient, nurturing, and self-sacrificing. We are never supposed to lose our tempers or feel too tired to listen to our children. We must always know how to handle their problems and never have needs of our own that get in the way of meeting their needs. The reality is that mothering is hard work, and every mother is human. No woman could be expected to live up to the ideal all of the time. But how many off days are okay? In the absence of a clear answer, women strive for perfection.

It's hard for a woman to judge when she has done enough as a wife and mother. Most jobs have tangible outcomes: projects that need to be completed by a certain time, piles of paper to move from the in-box to the out-box, customers to be served, letters to be processed, or files to be closed. Seeing these outcomes gives us a sense of accomplishment. We can remember how big that pile on our desk was and feel good about getting through it. However, the achievements associated with the female gender role are fleeting: meals that take an hour to make take ten minutes to eat; clean houses are instantly untidy when children come home from school; clothes are dirty again after being worn once. The work associated with the female gender role is never really finished. As soon as one task is completed, another pops up to take its place. The big successes, like happy, well-adjusted children, are few and far between, and they are difficult to see early on. The never-ending nature of the work may add to a woman's feeling that she can't do enough.

In addition to being a difficult job, which it is impossible to finish or do well all the time, women's gender role is not highly valued. I read recently that having one parent stay at home with children is worth $55,000 U.S. in services to the family. Yet how often have you heard a stay-at-home mother referred to as "only" a mother? Success isn't measured by well-adjusted children and smoothly functioning households in our society; it is measured by salaries and promotions.

Women's gender role involves excelling at an unending task that is not highly valued. Some researchers believe this is why married women with children are at risk for depression. Indeed, in cultures where women's role in the family is highly valued, women are at lower risk.

BRINGING HOME BABY

No experience makes a woman more aware of her gender role than having a baby. Some women who are going through postpartum depression seem to be collapsing under the weight of the role. They feel overwhelmed by the responsibility of motherhood and inadequately prepared for it. They think about their relationship with their own mother, and, whether that relationship was good or bad, they are afraid they will never be good enough. Often they are married to men who don't participate in housework or child care, don't support their efforts to be good mothers, and leave them feeling inadequate and alone. In my clinical experience, husbands often feel overwhelmed by fatherhood themselves, but this isn't obvious to their wives who see only that their husbands throw themselves into work outside the home.

This is part of what Tracy felt. She felt overwhelmed by looking after her son. She was frustrated by being unable to get much done during a day. Some women would say she was doing well if she could look after the baby and accomplish one other chore, but Tracy wasn't satisfied. Matt didn't pitch in. When he didn't take over some of Tracy's chores, he gave her the message that she should be able to do it all. Like a lot of new fathers, he would arrive home in the evening to an untidy house and no dinner and he'd ask what she had done all day.

Matt also seems to fit the picture we have of postpartum depression in that he seemed preoccupied with his job and disinterested in Tracy and their son. His apparent disinterest led Tracy to conclude that he didn't love her and regretted having the baby with her. But I suspected he was as overwhelmed by fatherhood as she was by motherhood. After some couple therapy sessions, Tracy learned that Matt worked constantly in part because he felt the pressure of his gender role to provide for his family. New fathers often feel shut out by the close relationship between their partner and the baby. They don't know how to be part of that relationship, so they turn to work, which is something they do know.

Gender roles help us to understand part of why Tracy was depressed. However, this isn't her whole story, as we will see in later chapters.

SILENCING THE SELF

Some researchers have looked to the personality traits that society encourages in girls and women as an explanation for women's greater depression. These researchers wonder if these traits put women at risk. Interestingly, positive traits like empathy and warmth are not associated with depression. However, women whose personalities are extremely oriented toward caring for other people do experience more depression (Helgeson 1994).

A psychologist named Dana Jack (1991) interviewed a dozen women who were depressed then spoke with them again once their episodes were over. She asked them to talk about their depression and how they had come to feel this way. Her findings were published in a book called *Silencing the Self*, which I often recommend to the depressed women I treat because it provides a picture of depression that closely matches their experience.

For eleven of the twelve women Jack interviewed, depression was a response to significant problems in their relationships, particularly with their husbands. These women described their marriages as cold and distant, but they felt unable to leave because they were financially dependent. Ten of the twelve women did not work outside the home.

The Good Wife

These women had strong beliefs about what it meant to be a "good" wife and mother. They used words like "unselfish," "giving," and "self-sacrificing" to describe the ideal woman, and they equated success as a wife and mother with taking care of people. They constantly put the needs of their husbands and children ahead of their own needs, often to the point of self-sacrifice. They believed that if they were good enough caregivers, their families would be happy and loving. However, self-sacrifice did not result in the ideal family they hoped for. Instead, their relationships were unhappy and their families did not value their efforts. Because they believed they were responsible for making relationships work, they blamed themselves for this "failure" and put even more effort into being good wives and mothers.

Most women try to meet the needs of others to some extent. However, the only way to do this constantly is by ignoring our own needs. Over time, the women Jack interviewed began to feel frustrated and resentful that their needs were never met. Outwardly they seemed to go along with their family's demands, but inside they were seething. They worried that expressing their frustration would lead to conflict, so they did not say what they really thought or how they really felt. They feared that if their husbands and families knew how angry they were, they would be abandoned. They believed they had to make a choice:

they could silence themselves and stay in the relationship or speak their mind and lose it.

For these women, depression set in when they realized that no matter how hard they tried, they would never succeed. Their sacrifices had been made in vain. Giving up, admitting defeat, accepting that their marriages and families would never be what they wanted led the women to become depressed.

My Mother, Myself

Many of these women had grown up watching their own mothers defer to their fathers. They rarely saw their parents fight, but they did not see the effort their mothers made to avoid conflict with their fathers. Conflict is a normal part of an intimate relationship, but these women didn't know that. Conflict must mean they had failed.

LISA

Lisa grew up in this kind of family. She described her father as a successful businessman and her mother as easily intimidated by her better-educated, more intelligent, and more forceful husband. Lisa's mother never challenged her husband's authority. Lisa remembered a time when she was about eight years old and her father was extremely angry with her. In a temper, he kicked her small dog. The dog yelped and ran away to hide, and Lisa was sent to her room, wailing. After her father left the house, her mother took Lisa from her room and together they took the dog to the vet. Their trip was a secret that Lisa's mother made her promise she would never tell her father.

Lisa already believed that her father was smarter than her mother. Her mother's behavior in this situation told her that even when a husband isn't being smart, even when he is clearly wrong, he should not be challenged. She carried this belief into her own marriage. Lisa's husband, David, often drank heavily on Saturday nights. On Sunday afternoon, hungover and grumpy, he would fall asleep on the living room couch. The children had no other room to play in, but if they woke him up with their noise he would yell at Lisa that she was a lousy mother for not keeping them quiet. Lisa knew that one solution was to ask David to take his naps in their bedroom. Instead, she put the children in their rooms and warned them not to make any noise that could wake their father. Lisa knew her solution wasn't fair to the children, and she worried about the message she was giving them, but her fears for them weren't great enough to risk a confrontation with David.

Lisa had a clear idea of what a good wife should be. She included being a "sex object" in her definition. She believed she had to tolerate David's sexual treatment of her even though it felt humiliating. When I first met her, she had never told him how she felt about their sexual relationship. Like the women in Jack's book, Lisa sacrificed her own sexual needs to meet what she thought were his needs. However, doing so did not bring intimacy with him. In fact, sex usually ended with him sleeping in the spare bedroom.

My Parents, Myself

Not all of the depressed women I've treated grew up in homes with a dominant father and a submissive mother.

ANNE

Anne remembered her mother as an outgoing, vibrant, and willful woman. Her father was warm and loving, especially to Anne. Her parents were not happy together, but religious beliefs prevented them from divorcing. They fought constantly. Throughout Anne's childhood, they had open battles in which the children often participated. When Anne married, she was determined to avoid conflict with her husband, no matter what the cost.

Anne described herself as an attractive, sociable, and "dramatic" young woman who loved being the center of attention. At parties, she laughed and drank too much; she danced and flirted with other women's husbands. Bill was a serious young man who preferred reading to parties. He was attracted to Anne's warmth and drama at first, but he soon found her behavior "silly" and embarrassing. He scolded her to "grow up" and act like an adult. Anne knew there was some truth to what Bill said. She knew that sometimes she drank too much and got out of hand. She wanted to be the wife he wanted, so she toned herself down. She traded in her brightly colored hippie clothes for the matched sweater sets and pearls that Bill liked. She tried to become more serious and "rational." She spent her evenings reading literature instead of flipping through fashion magazines or chatting on the phone with her girlfriends.

But no matter how hard Anne tried and no matter what she changed about herself, Bill's approval always seemed to be just around the corner. As the years passed, she didn't get any closer to him. In fact, the more she suppressed the real Anne, the more distant the marriage became. After several years, she realized the marriage was a disaster, but by that time she had no idea where she would go or what she would do without him. Her primary confidante was her sister, but Anne didn't want to tell her sister about her marital problems. They often joked about their parents' marriage, and she was embarrassed to admit that hers was no better. After a while, she could no longer tell if her unhappiness was due to her cold, distant marriage or to her own "neediness," as Bill repeatedly labeled her feelings. Without someone to talk to, she didn't know if she should leave him or not. So she did what Bill had always suggested: she transferred her energy to the theater, where she became an amateur actress.

Anne was not depressed during these years, although she sometimes felt down and lonely. She was not truly depressed until Bill did what she had always feared: he left her. Anne was incensed. Breaking down into furious tears in a therapy session, she told me she was angry with him because she had "paid her dues, played the dutiful wife, and I should not be left alone at fifty years of age, the shamed and failed wife."

DOES GENDER ROLE EXPLAIN DEPRESSION?

Many of the women I work with tell me their romantic relationships are cold and distant. They describe a gradual breakdown in their relations with their partners, which begins with their feeling criticized and devalued. They try harder to be good wives. They suppress angry thoughts and feelings. They put aside their own needs to meet what they think might be their partner's needs. For a while, silencing themselves seems to improve the situation, but it is always a temporary solution. If we cannot be genuine in an intimate relationship, there can be no real intimacy. The relationship grows colder and more distant, which we will see in chapter 8 can be very painful both for the depressed woman and for her partner. Although self-silencing is not the whole story, as we will learn for both Lisa and Anne, Jack provides a compelling description of many depressed women's lives.

Obviously, caring for others is not inherently bad. Many women who have never experienced depression recognize themselves in Jack's description. Mothers, in particular, believe that putting their needs aside is an essential part of motherhood. Indeed, we all pity the child of a woman who doesn't put her needs aside. However, people need to choose when and what they give, and they need to feel that their giving is appreciated and returned. When women experience caring for their families as an obligation and not as something they choose, they are at risk for depression.

In my clinical experience, gender roles are linked to depression because girls and women want to have close, harmonious relationships. Relationships are protective when they are healthy and secure, but clearly they are detrimental when they are conflicted and insecure. The fact that women care about their relationships makes them vulnerable to depression when those relationships go wrong.

Questions to Ask Yourself

1. How fairly are housework and child care divided between my partner and me? Does this division of labor bother me?

2. Do I think I need to sacrifice myself to show people that I care? Do I constantly put others' needs ahead of mine?

3. What is a "good wife"? What is a "good mother"? How do I measure up to these ideals?

4. Do I sometimes feel angry with the people I take care of because I think they don't appreciate me or don't realize how much I do for them?

5. Do I tell them when I'm angry with them? If not, what would happen if I did?

6. What was my mother's role in the family? What is my role in my family? What did I learn from her about being a wife and/or mother?

7. What was my parents' marriage like when I was a kid? What is my romantic relationship or marriage like? What did I learn about intimate relationships from watching my parents (good and bad)?

CHAPTER 5

families: unhappy in their own ways

In the book *Anna Karenina*, the Russian author Leo Tolstoy wrote that all happy families resemble one another but that each unhappy family is unique. As a writer, Tolstoy was attuned to the infinite varieties of unhappiness. Families may be overwhelmed by parental mental illness or alcoholism, by marital conflict, violence, chronic illness, or the death of a child. They can collapse under the weight of bad luck, financial problems, or poverty. As a psychotherapist, I am aware that every unhappy woman who comes into my office has a unique story to tell. As a research psychologist, I know there are similarities among unhappy families. They have common ways of communicating and dealing with conflict that increase children's risk for depression.

Based on our experiences in our families, we create a picture of the world. We use this picture to guide our understanding of what happens to us in relationships outside the family and to form expectations for how we will be treated. A child who is rejected, ignored, or abused in her family will go into the world expecting more of the same. Parents who are rejecting, critical, uncaring, or authoritarian create children who are at risk for depression.

When I talk about individual parents in this chapter, I refer to the child as female and the parent as male to simplify my writing. However, what I say applies to both mothers and fathers.

WHO DID YOU GO TO?

All of us have times we are hurt, unhappy, sad, fearful, or stressed. These emotions are a normal part of life. Children's emotions are more intense than adults' emotions, and unlike adults, children have fewer strategies for handling feelings on their own. Without help, children's emotions can easily spiral out of control.

When women first come to see me, I always ask, "When you were little and you hurt yourself or got upset, who did you go to?" Clients in their 30s, 40s, and 50s are puzzled by this question. They ask, "What does that have to do with how I feel now?" When I ask if they can tell me anyway, the answer is usually "No one." One woman went to her room. Another escaped to the garden with her cats. Some women say they might have tried talking to one of their parents, but often the parent was too busy or stressed to pay attention. Some women don't remember getting upset as children. They tell me nothing really bothered them until suddenly as adults they started to feel depressed.

Most of us handle negative feelings at least in part by turning to the people we feel closest to and most trust. The people we love provide comfort and reassurance. Sometimes they help us solve a problem; sometimes their touch is enough to make us feel better. Nowhere is this more apparent than between children and the people who care for them. A parent's kiss really does make a scraped knee feel better. Children who have no one to turn to have not experienced the healing touch of another person's care. They feel alone in dealing with whatever life throws at them.

ATTACHMENT THEORY: FROM THE CRADLE TO THE GRAVE

Attachment theory was developed by a British psychiatrist, John Bowlby (1969, 1973, 1980), who worked extensively with young children. He observed that children first learn about relationships through their experiences with the people who look after them, usually their parents. In these early relationships, children learn whether they are lovable or inadequate, whether other people are helpful or angry, and whether they will be treated well or poorly. The parent-child relationship sets the stage for all that follows. What a child learns about herself and other people from her parents is likely to be with her "from the cradle to the grave" (Bowlby 1969, 208).

Bowlby saw that babies seem to be programmed to form close relationships with the people who look after them. When babies are about nine months old, they start to be distressed by strangers. This reaction is even more intense when they are separated from the person who normally takes care of them. The baby will cry and appear to protest the separation. When she is reunited with her caregiver, she seems relieved. She may smile and make happy noises or try to make contact with the caregiver. Bowlby pointed out that it is adaptive for babies and young children to form attachments to the people who look after them. The world is a dangerous place; a young child needs someone close by who will look out for her and protect her from harm. Although this person is normally a parent, anyone who looks after the child regularly can be an attachment figure: a grandparent, a foster parent, a babysitter, or even a teacher.

Babies form attachments to each person who looks after them. The nature of the attachment depends on how the adult typically responds when the baby is in need. Babies get tired, hungry, and thirsty; their stomachs hurt and their bottoms chap. But they are helpless to make themselves feel better. They cannot even describe the problem. All they can do is signal their distress by crying and hope their parents notice. It is up to parents to figure out when children are in need and how to meet those needs. A parent who responds quickly and is able to identify and solve the problem shows the baby that others care about her needs and will try to meet them. When a parent is preoccupied and ignores the baby's crying, yells at her to stop, or can't figure out what the child needs and gives up, that parent shows the baby that other people cannot be counted on to make her feel better.

The baby's *temperament* also plays a part in how the attachment relationship develops (Belsky and Rovine 1987). Temperament is the part of our personality that is present from birth. One aspect of temperament is stress reactivity. While some babies are calm and easygoing, others are easily upset and have difficulty calming down. The latter type of baby is said to have a *difficult temperament*. Difficult babies cry a lot, and they need a lot of soothing from their parents. They may need to be held and rocked more than a baby with an easier temperament. Babies with a difficult temperament can have a negative impact on their caregivers. For instance, the mothers of these babies often are irritable with and critical of their infants. A temperamentally difficult baby may challenge the parent's ability to be a warm and responsive caregiver, particularly if the parent also is someone who is easily stressed.

For young children, the major purpose of an attachment relationship is to keep the child safe and cared for physically. A child whose basic needs are met is free to explore her environment and to develop as an individual. Children whose basic needs are not met may be inhibited by anxiety. They will not have the basic emotional security needed to venture into the world and find out what it is all about.

The Changing Face of Attachment

As children mature, their attachment needs change. An older child does not need to be fed every few hours, but she does need help with her homework. She needs to learn how to swim and ride a bike. She needs to be taken to playdates. She needs someone to talk her through her frustration as she learns something new and difficult. Children rely on their caregivers, both to meet their physical needs and to cope with the complex world in which they live.

Children also turn to their parents to meet their emotional needs. When they are upset, children who have a good attachment relationship go to their parents for reassurance and comfort. Parents help a child to handle her emotions, in part by soothing her and in part by helping the child learn how to soothe herself. Children often do not know what they are feeling or why, particularly when they are upset. Parents help by talking to children about their feelings and about the situation that has upset them. In this way, parents provide children with a way of understanding the stormy and sometimes overwhelming feelings they have. Often knowing what we feel and why we feel it is reassuring, even if the problem is still there.

The purpose of attachment has changed. While older children still rely on parents to meet their basic needs for safety and physical care, increasingly the parent is a source of emotional support, especially for girls and women. As I discuss later in this chapter, when girls do not have good attachment relationships they are at risk for depression.

Can I Count On You?

According to attachment theory, when a child is stressed, uncertain, or upset, she looks to her caregivers to see if they can be counted on to provide the comfort, support, and help she needs. The answer to the question "Can I count on you?" is a significant factor in how she feels about herself and how trusting she is of other people.

A child who is *securely attached* is confident that the answer to the question "Can I count on you?" is "Yes." Her parents respond to her physical and emotional needs. They may not be able to solve all her problems or always give her what she wants, but she feels understood. Her needs are taken into account. Her parents are warm and loving and interested in her, which teaches her that she is lovable and important, the basis of self-esteem.

As a securely attached child becomes an adolescent and young adult, she will develop good relationships with other people who are important to her, like friends and romantic partners. She will have good social skills, and she will know how to deal with conflict in ways that strengthen rather than weaken her relationships. When she feels unhappy, she will have people to turn to and she will be able to take the comfort and help they offer to cope with negative events in her life.

Although securely attached girls can become depressed when bad things happen to them, they are likely to recover quickly because they believe in themselves and they are able to use the support available to them to feel better and to solve their problems. In my clinical work, I rarely see depressed women whose attachment style is secure. Securely attached women usually do not need the help of a psychotherapist to cope with depression.

The child for whom the answer to the question "Can I count on you?" is "No" is said to be *insecurely attached*. Insecurely attached children have learned they cannot count on the people who look after them to respond to their physical and/or emotional needs.

In a happy family, a child is likely to be securely attached to both parents. In an unhappy one, she may be securely attached to one parent but not to the other or she may be insecurely attached to both parents.

Insecure Attachment: Turning Up the Volume

There are two basic patterns of insecure attachment. Which one develops depends on the parent's behavior.

In the first pattern, the child's parent is often angry or impatient with her, and at times he may be outright rejecting. A rejecting parent finds many things to criticize in his child. He may blame her when things go wrong. He may use derogatory language, like telling her she is "useless" or "stupid," particularly when she makes a mistake. Rejection also can be subtle. He may communicate his disappointment without words but leave no doubt in the child's mind that she is not good enough or that she has not lived up to his expectations.

A rejected child accepts her parent's view of her as the truth, and as a result she sees herself as flawed and bad. She may experience intense feelings of shame, especially when she makes a mistake. However, she also struggles against this picture, in part because no one wants to feel they are bad and in part because she knows that sometimes her parents are wrong.

Rejected children feel a lot of anger and resentment, not only toward their parents but toward other people as well. They have difficulties with people in authority, who they expect will criticize and reject them. They have trouble controlling their anger, especially when they get into conflicts with people they care about. At the same time, they often feel emotionally needy. They may seek constant advice, care, and support from people who are close to them. Parents, grandparents, and teachers may feel that no matter how much love, care, and support rejected children are given, it is never enough.

These are children who have *turned up the volume* when it comes to their attachment needs. They demand loudly and insistently that their parents pay attention to them, and when their parents don't, they are enraged. They may cry and yell when they are disappointed by their parents. Or they may express anger indirectly by disobeying rules and talking back.

The sad irony of this strategy is that it turns off the very people from whom the rejected child wants comfort. The parents feel attacked and criticized. They feel incapable of doing enough to satisfy her. They feel helpless to cope with her anger. The relationship that is so important to her is filled with conflict and disappointment.

Adolescent girls who are clinically depressed are highly likely to have this kind of relationship with their parents (Rosenstein and Horowitz 1996). They are very worried that their parents are going to abandon them. Often these fears are justified.

I was asked to do a psychological assessment of a Native American girl who had been adopted by Caucasian parents. Julie was about twelve years old, and she had a younger sister who was the couple's biological child. Julie had been having temper tantrums at home and school, but her parents were more concerned about what they labeled her "criminal" behavior. As an example, they told me she had cleaned out the garage for them and pocketed the money she got for the empty pop bottles when she returned them. They felt this incident reflected her aboriginal background. They didn't want her to "corrupt" their younger daughter, and they clearly wanted me to recommend that she be placed in foster care.

I met with Julie to talk with her and to give her some tests. Not surprisingly, Julie was depressed. She was also sullen, angry, and uncooperative, and it took me some time to gain her trust. At the end of our meeting I asked if she had any questions. She turned to me with huge tear-filled eyes and asked, "Are my parents trying to give me back?" Of course, they were. Julie's fears that she would be abandoned had led her to act out angrily against her parents, which justified her parents' rejection of her.

Insecure Attachment: Turning Down the Volume

The second kind of insecure attachment occurs when parents are emotionally distant, self-absorbed, and disinterested in the child. The indifferent parent may be too wrapped up in his own life or problems to pay attention to his child. He may be bored by her conversation. He may be uncomfortable with physical closeness and so reject the child's hugs and kisses. The indifferent parent may meet the child's basic physical needs, but he is disinterested in spending time with her, talking with her, and doing things she likes. When he does something kind for her, it is because being kind makes him feel good as a parent, not because his kindness is what the child needs. Often these gestures are misplaced.

The child of an indifferent parent learns that she and her needs are not important. She may feel she is less interesting, less intelligent, and less worthy than her parent. Often this child will understand her parent's indifference as meaning that he doesn't care for her. However, because the parent meets her material needs and may even indulge them, she may feel confused and guilty about this perception.

The child whose parent is indifferent to her is most likely to *turn down the volume* when it comes to her emotional needs. She lowers her expectations of other people and learns not to make demands on them. She learns to handle her own problems and feelings so that she does not have to count on others. The less she talks about her feelings, the less aware of them she is. This is a relief when the feelings are bad. Eventually she may rarely be aware of what she is feeling, good or bad.

There are two basic problems with this strategy for coping with an indifferent parent. The first is that it pushes people away. Other people see these children as cold and distant, which virtually guarantees their continued isolation.

The strategy of muting the volume also distances the child from her own feelings. Bad feelings signal that something is wrong. These children can stay in negative or even harmful situations, like friendships where they are taken advantage of or abusive relationships, because they are out of touch with how bad the situation makes them feel.

Because these children are well behaved and obedient, they are unlikely to be seen as depressed by their parents and teachers. Because they have shut down their bad feelings, they are unlikely to feel depressed. Often they become aware of their depression only as adults, when they are confronted with evidence of their parent's indifference.

One woman I worked with put her energy into school and did so well that she eventually became a physician. As an adult she also cared for her chronically ill mother, despite having a child of her own and a busy career. She had sole responsibility for her mother because her only sibling, a brother, was a drug addict and criminal who usually was either hiding from the police or in jail. She came to see me after her mother made an offhand comment that devastated her. Her mother told her that she never gave much thought to her daughter, but that she felt a special connection to her son. "He's in my womb," she told her daughter. With this sentence, the mother confirmed what my client had always suspected: she and her efforts were invisible to her mother.

WHOSE NEEDS ARE MORE IMPORTANT?

Attachment theory emphasizes the universal need to feel loved, nurtured, comforted, and supported. Most parents know that children need to be loved. But as parents they think they also are responsible for raising children who are mature, cooperative, and productive members of society. They try to teach moral values, self-discipline, and good work habits. The child's need for love and the parent's need to produce a certain kind of child can, at times, come into conflict. A psychologist named Diana Baumrind (1989) is interested in how parents balance these competing needs. She has identified three basic parenting styles: authoritative, permissive, and authoritarian.

The Authoritative Parent

Authoritative parents are warm and loving. They expect their child to be a mature and cooperative member of the family, but they are aware of and responsive to the child as an individual as well. When the parent's interests conflict with those of the child, these parents normally discuss the issue. Take, for instance, a disagreement about music lessons. The parent thinks the child should learn to play a musical instrument, but the child wants to quit her piano lessons. The authoritative parent would explain why he thinks music lessons are important. However, he would also find out what the child doesn't like about them. The authoritative parent takes the child's perspective into account in reaching a balance between what he sees as important and what the child considers important. He may give up his goal to have the child play a musical instrument if he learns that she has no talent for it. Or they could reach a compromise that achieves the goals he has for her while keeping her interests and needs in mind. Maybe she would rather play the flute or sing.

In our society, this parenting style has the best outcomes for children. Authoritative families tend to be close and to experience little parent-child conflict. This may seem surprising because asking for the child's viewpoint may seem to open the door to disagreement. In fact, when children feel they are heard and their needs are taken into account, they are more cooperative. The children in these families see their parents as loving, and they feel securely attached to them. They are generally happy with life. They are mature and considerate of other people. They feel good about themselves and capable of meeting the challenges set for them at school and home.

The Permissive Parent

The permissive parent puts the emphasis on meeting the child's needs. He makes few demands on her. He tends not to have very high expectations for her and he rarely punishes her misbehavior. He would let her quit the piano lessons, without question. The children of permissive parents do not have much self-control, and they do not do well in areas of life that require self-discipline, like school and work. However, while they may have other emotional problems, these children are not at particular risk for depression.

The Authoritarian Parent

The authoritarian parent puts his goals for the child ahead of the child's goals for herself. He wants the child's behavior to conform to some ideal standard. Often these standards involve moral behavior or achievement at school or work. These parents could be trying to give their children a better life than they had. Their own upbringing or culture could have forged strong beliefs about what children should and should not do. These parents have clear and, often, high expectations for their children, and they believe there should be consequences if children fail to meet these standards.

The authoritarian parent expects to be obeyed without question. When the parent's and child's needs conflict, the authoritarian parent does not encourage the child to discuss her point of view. He expects to be obeyed. If the child disobeys him, he punishes her, often by withdrawing his love. The authoritarian parent would insist the child continue the lessons without finding out why she wants to quit or looking for a compromise.

Of the three parenting styles, this one is the least positive for children. Authoritarian parents are less supportive of their children, and the children are less inclined to see them as loving, so they are more likely to feel insecurely attached. These families also experience more conflict. Although the children of authoritarian parents are generally well behaved, some disagreement between parents and children is inevitable. These families have difficulty resolving conflict because of the parent's unwillingness to take the child's view into account. Despite these problems, the children of authoritarian parents can do well, particularly at school. However, the boys are often angry; the girls may be submissive and dependent on others.

Not all children of authoritarian parents are at risk for depression. The critical factor is how much warmth the child experiences in her relationship with the authoritarian parent. A strict parent who clearly expresses love for his child is one thing; one who chews out his daughter when she doesn't meet his expectations is another. However, authoritarian parents often do not express love for their children. They may come from a culture that values emotional self-control. Or being "tough" could be part of what the parent is trying to teach the child, as is often the case with parents whose kids are heavily involved in sports. When the authoritarian parent is also cold and punitive, the child is likely to experience depression (Kim et al. 2003). Thus, authoritarian parenting is most likely to result in depression for the child when it is combined with insecure attachment.

GROW WHERE YOU'RE PLANTED

Children try to grow wherever they're planted. The conditions may not be right. The soil may be poor and there may not be enough sunlight, but the child will do her best to grow in the conditions she has been given.

Children learn to adapt to their parents. A child who turns up the volume will sometimes get the attention she craves. A child who turns off her emotional needs has recognized that the parent is not going to respond. Both insecure attachment strategies are the child's way of adapting to her parent. They are highly useful as long as the child lives with her parents and often only become a problem when they are generalized to new relationships, where they are neither appropriate nor accurate. For instance, as I will show in chapter 6, a child who has learned to turn off her needs and become self-reliant may not know how to get support when she needs it.

Insecure attachment is often a blind spot for the depressed women I see in therapy. As children, they probably believed that the way their parents treated them was the same way other parents treated their children. Unless their own parent's behavior was extreme, they would have no reason to believe their experience was not normal. Children also have no choice about their parents. Adults can choose to leave romantic partners who make them feel bad; children do not have that luxury. When there is no choice, it is often adaptive to make the best of the situation, and making the best of it may include ignoring or not thinking about how the parent's behavior is hurtful.

Even if they are less than terrific parents, most parents of insecurely attached children are not bad people. They differ from the parents of securely attached children in a very specific way: they are not responsive enough to their children's needs. Not all parents are equally sensitive. Not all parents are comfortable enough with their own needs to be responsive to those of their children. Parents can learn to be more sensitive and responsive to their children. This is not usually an unfixable defect but an aspect of the parent's personality that has a negative and often unintended impact on their children.

Many rejecting or indifferent parents are not like this all the time. Most are *inconsistent*. An inconsistent parent is sometimes warm and engaged, sometimes cold and detached, sometimes playful and easygoing, and sometimes rigid and harsh. Many inconsistent parents can be warm and engaged as long as they do not feel stressed. They react to stress by becoming self-absorbed and easily irritated by things that normally would not bother them. In some ways, having an inconsistent parent is worse than having a parent who is always rejecting or indifferent because it may be easy for the child to blame herself for the parent's inconsistency. She may think her parent is only rejecting or detached when she doesn't behave properly.

UNHAPPY MARRIAGES MAKE UNHAPPY FAMILIES

Parents are more likely to be rejecting, disengaged, authoritarian, and inconsistent when they are unhappily married (Krishnakumar and Buehler 2000). Marital problems create a general negative mood in the home that spills over into the parents' relationships with their children. A parent who is already irritated with his wife is likely to blow up when one of his children misbehaves.

When couples are fighting, they also are unable to support each other as parents. Parents who work well together give each other feedback about their parenting (Kobak and Mandelbaum 2003). Often one parent understands some aspect of the child's behavior that the other does not. When one parent is being unreasonable or has overly high expectations for the child, the other parent can point this out. Happily married couples reach a consensus about who their children are and how best to parent them. When parents are fighting, feedback usually is taken as criticism. The child can become another topic to fight about or another example of the different ways in which the partners see the world.

When parents fight a lot, the family tends to be less close and less flexible, which is linked to depression in both sons and daughters. However, girls are more vulnerable than boys to all kinds of family stress and conflict. So it is not surprising that girls are particularly at risk for depression when their parents are unhappily married.

One possible reason is that marital distress changes the daughter's relationships with her parents. Unhappily married fathers withdraw from their families, especially from their daughters. They may spend long hours at work and be uncommunicative when they are home. A father's apparent lack of interest in his daughter may increase her attachment insecurity in her relationship with him. In contrast, an unhappily married mother often turns to her daughter for emotional support. Daughters who are busy giving support may not get enough themselves. Some mothers discuss their marital problems with their daughters and try to draw their daughters into an alliance against the father. This leaves the daughter feeling enmeshed in her parents' problems and alienated from her father.

Unfortunately, children usually do not know that their parents are angry, rejecting, detached, and authoritarian because they are unhappily married. Children see things almost exclusively from their own point of view, so a child who feels rejected or overlooked by a parent is most likely to conclude there is something wrong with her. One of the important tasks of therapy with adult women is helping them to understand that much of what their parents did while they were children had little to do with them and a great deal to do with who their parents were and the lives they were living.

WHY INSECURE ATTACHMENT AND AUTHORITARIAN PARENTING LEAD TO DEPRESSION

Insecure attachment leads children to believe they are not worthy of love and care (Roberts, Gotlib, and Kassel 1996). They have low self-esteem and a low opinion of their ability to accomplish things in life. They feel inadequate. Low self-esteem is not just a symptom of depression; it contributes to feelings of depression. When you believe that your parents do not love or like you and that you can never be good enough for them, depression is probably inevitable.

When insecurely attached children and adolescents feel stressed, they are unlikely to turn to other people for emotional support (Shirk, Gudmundsen, and Burwell 2005). A child whose parents were unresponsive is unlikely to think that other people might be there for her when she needs them. Expecting others to respond to her as her parents have done, the insecurely attached child or adolescent tries to cope with her difficulties on her own. This coping strategy prevents her from getting help that could be useful and leaves her feeling alone and isolated, which increases her risk for depression.

A lot of the stress in our lives is interpersonal. People are stressed by conflicts with others or by what they perceive as rejection. A girl who is securely attached may be able to brush off interpersonal difficulties or to see them as specific problems to be overcome. However, a girl who is insecurely attached may interpret interpersonal difficulties as confirming that she is unworthy and unlovable (Hammen et al. 1995).

Insecurely attached girls (Roberts, Gotlib, and Kassel 1996) and those whose parents are authoritarian (Soenens et al. 2005) also believe that their worth as a person depends on their ability to meet very specific standards. For instance, they believe it is important to have the approval of other people, with the result that they are overly concerned about what other people think of them. One depressed woman I worked with called this her "invisible chorus." She went through life imagining a group of people standing behind her, holding up numbers as they judged the adequacy of her performance. These children also believe that unless they are perfect, people will not love them. This belief puts pressure on them never to make mistakes. They set unrealistic standards and goals for themselves and beat themselves up when they fail to meet them.

No one's behavior has the full approval of everyone all the time. No one can go through life without making mistakes. When people who expect approval and perfection fall short of this goal, they are at risk for depression.

ANNE: *TURNING UP THE VOLUME*

Anne had a close relationship with her father. However, he was often not available to her because he and her mother would fight and he would "disappear" into his workshop. A loving parent who is not physically present cannot provide the basis for secure attachment.

From early on, Anne felt that her mother was warm and nurturing with her sister Debbie but not with her. For instance, when Anne was about fifteen, she went out with Debbie one summer night to meet a boy Debbie liked. The sisters lied to their mother about where they were going because they were not allowed to date boys. To meet the boy they had to borrow a car, which they got from a girlfriend of Anne's. When the sisters got home, their mother was waiting for them. Under cross-examination they admitted where they had been. Then, to Anne's astonishment, Debbie was sent to bed. Her mother called Anne a "slut" and a "juvenile delinquent" for driving the car without a license. Only she was grounded.

Anne tried to avoid conflict with her mother, but with the personalities involved, conflict was inevitable. Anne learned to lie to avoid getting into trouble. When she was caught, Anne's deception confirmed her mother's view of her as willful and disobedient. Her mother may have genuinely believed that the only reason her "good daughter" lied and borrowed a car to visit a boy was because she was under the influence of her "bad daughter." If Anne's parents had been more happily married, her father might have been able to give her mother the feedback that she was being unfair to Anne. However, he seems to have stayed out of their arguments.

As a woman, Anne still showed many of the characteristics of a rejected child. She was easily angered by her husband, her work colleagues, and even by me. She had great difficulty with people having authority over her. Her power struggles with her boss were so intense that she lost her job. Although I did not work with Anne and her husband in couple therapy, Anne's anger likely contributed to their marital problems.

At the same time, Anne could be intensely dependent. She made many emotional demands on her sister. When she was upset, she would telephone Debbie, who lived a three-hour drive away, and ask to be picked up. She would stay at Debbie's home for as long as a week even though her sister was married with adolescent children. If Debbie was too busy to come get her, Anne would accuse her sister of not caring about her. Often Debbie would become angry because she felt she bent over backward to support Anne and accommodate her needs. Anne was doomed either way. Not getting what she wanted from her sister was a painful reminder of her mother's rejection, but Debbie's constant attention confirmed Anne's view of herself as helpless, dependent, and needy.

One day Anne called me from her home, which was a fifteen-minute walk from my office. She told me she was unable to come to my office for our appointment, and she asked that I go to her house instead. I explained that it would be better for her to get dressed and come to my office. She did as I asked. However, she was furious with me when she arrived. She accused me of not caring about her and of being interested only in the money she paid for our sessions.

I had to avoid the trap of becoming defensive and angry myself and in that way confirming her belief that I would reject her. Instead, I used this situation as an opportunity to explore Anne's rage whenever she was let down. I let her talk about her anger with me without accepting responsibility for having caused it. Talking about her anger helped her calm down. As she settled down, Anne began to realize she had unrealistic expectations about others meeting her needs. When we speculated about why she might have these expectations, she linked the feeling that she deserved to be cared for back to her mother. She said she was very angry with her mother for the way she had been treated, especially in contrast to Debbie. She expected Debbie to make it up to her by giving her what their mother had not. Anne realized it was not reasonable to expect Debbie to drive three hours to pick her up when Anne could easily drive herself.

Learning to distinguish which of our emotional reactions come from the past and which are due to what is happening in the present is an important step in therapy.

In her birth family, Anne had been criticized and rejected, so when her husband Bill told her she was silly and frivolous, she accepted his criticism as valid. She stayed in a marriage where she was not valued because not being valued was what she expected. Bill's criticism confirmed what she had always believed about herself: she was defective and unworthy of his love.

As a child, Anne also learned to be more concerned about what other people thought of her than about her own happiness. She did not want to admit to her sister that her marriage was unhappy because she was afraid Debbie would look down on her. She expected to have a perfect marriage, and when the marriage was clearly wrong for her, she stayed in it long past the point many women would have because she did not want to see herself as a failure. Anne became depressed when Bill left her because the reality of her bad marriage could no longer be hidden.

LISA: *TURNING DOWN THE VOLUME*

Lisa's parents were authoritarian. Earlier, I described them as a couple with traditional attitudes toward gender roles. They also were very religious, and they had high expectations for their two daughters. Not only were the girls expected to do well at school, they were expected to behave like proper young ladies. They were punished severely if they let their parents down.

One day Lisa was ready for church before the rest of her family. She was told to go outside and play while she waited. Predictably, she got her white socks and good dress dirty. Her parents punished her by making her stay home while the rest of the family attended services. Although this may not seem like much of a punishment, Lisa's parents knew she was afraid to be alone in the house. Lisa told me she crouched on her bed praying for her family to return. She had been terrified something terrible would happen and she would never see them again.

When I asked Lisa who she went to as a child when she was hurt or scared, she told me neither parent was a source of comfort. She was afraid of the dark and often woke in the night alone in her bedroom, but she was too afraid of her parents to go to them for comfort. Lisa saw them as both authoritarian and cold. The authoritarian parent always risks communicating his disinterest in his child's needs because he puts his own goals for her ahead of her own. Authoritarian parents also often punish their children by withdrawing their love, as Lisa's parents did.

Lisa met her parents' expectations for her at school, but she was a timid and sad child. She turned down the volume as a way of coping with her parents' inability to meet her needs. Turning down the volume with an authoritarian parent makes sense because disagreements create conflict and conflict is punished. The best way to avoid losing the connection to an authoritarian parent is for the child to make herself as small and unnoticeable as possible.

Lisa had no friends apart from the little dog that was her constant companion. When she was upset, she would go to her grandmother (her mother's mother) who lived close by. But she would not seek comfort from her. Her grandmother would build her a tent out of kitchen chairs and a bed spread. Lisa would crawl inside the tent with her dog and her books, and she would stay there until she felt safe to come out. Sometimes her grandmother would pass sandwiches or cookies into the tent but she never asked why Lisa had come to her or what she was feeling. The grandmother's behavior helps us understand why Lisa's mother was not a sensitive parent. She likely mothered Lisa the same way she had been mothered.

Lisa learned to become self-reliant. When she was a teenager, she left home. However, self-reliance did not mean she no longer listened to her parents. Even in her adult relationship with them, she described them as demanding and punitive. Her father still thought he knew what was best for his daughters. He counseled them about their personal lives, asking for details and making suggestions that invaded their privacy. On the rare occasion she disagreed with him, he became cold and distant. Although his interference made her angry, she was mystified as to why she still looked at him with the eyes of a child.

"Even when I'm hating him," she told me, "I want him to love me."

Lisa carried what she learned in her birth family into her relationship with her husband. She never expressed her emotional needs to David. She did not tell him how she felt about his frequent absences from home, his infidelities, or his treatment of her. She asked virtually nothing of him, except that he pay the bills. When I asked why she didn't tell him how she felt, she looked at me in utter astonishment. I could tell the thought had never occurred to her. In part, David went on hurting her because he had no idea how she felt about his behavior.

This does not excuse him, because most men can figure out that their wives do not like them to have affairs. However, David may have believed that Lisa minded less than other women. The absence of intimacy in their marriage strengthened Lisa's belief that she could not trust anyone to respond to her needs, and it confirmed her fear that she would always be alone.

Lisa chose a husband who was very similar to her father. David and her father got along well. Both were intelligent, well-educated men with strong opinions. Lisa completely accepted David's authority, as she had accepted her father's. Even though she was desperately unhappy in her marriage, she met his expectations for her as a wife. Her house was spotless, her children well cared for, and David was serviced sexually no matter what the emotional cost.

In her birth family, Lisa had learned that her needs were unimportant and that they should be set aside to meet the needs of others. She also learned that it was important to have the approval of other people, particularly men. She endured a difficult marriage that most women would have tried to change or would have left long before David confessed that he had fathered another woman's child. Lisa became depressed when she found herself trapped in a marriage that she could neither bear nor leave without risking the unthinkable: her father's disapproval.

WHY PARENTS MATTER

Relationships with parents are important because they form the basis of how a child feels about herself and what she expects in her relationships with others. A securely attached child goes into the world confident that others will like her and willing to ask for what she needs because she believes others will respond. An insecurely attached child goes into the world with apprehension. She is not sure others will like her because she is not sure she is likeable. She expects to be treated the same way she has been treated by her parents. She accepts criticism, rejection, victimization, and abuse because it is what she is used to.

Questions to Ask Yourself

1. As a child, when I was hurt or upset, who did I go to?

2. As a child, was I securely or insecurely attached to my mother? What about my father? Was there anyone else who was important to me in this way?

3. Did I turn the volume up or down in my relationships with my parents?

4. How was it adaptive for me to do this?

5. Can I see the traces of attachment insecurity in my present relationships?

6. Which of the three parenting styles best describes my mother? My father?

7. What impact has this parenting style had on me?

8. Were my parents happily married? How did I feel when they had fights? What did I do?

9. Were my parents on the same page when it came to handling me or did they disagree?

CHAPTER 6

families that hurt: childhood neglect & physical abuse

Children begin by loving their parents; as they grow older they judge them; sometimes they forgive them.

—Oscar Wilde, *The Picture of Dorian Gray*

Without crazy parents, comedians would be at a loss for material. Woody Allen famously joked that when his parents found out he had been kidnapped, they rented out his room. Rodney Dangerfield said he knew his parents didn't like him because his bath toys were a toaster and a radio. The film *My Big Fat Greek Wedding* is one long joke about crazy families. In our society, it is normal to think your family is crazy. However, some families are not just crazy in a humorous way; they are crazy in ways that are harmful to children. Woody Allen and Rodney

Dangerfield are funny only because we know they are exaggerating. If parents really did show total disregard for a child's safety, we would consider them poor or even dangerous parents.

Some parenting violates society's norms and expectations. In this chapter I discuss physical abuse and neglect, which risk children's physical safety. In chapter 7, I talk about sexual abuse. Both types of maltreatment have an impact on children's risk for depression. Childhood maltreatment increases the amount of stress that women experience later in life. Maltreatment also makes women wary of others, which prevents them from getting the support they need to cope with stress. Together these factors may explain why women with a history of childhood maltreatment are at risk for depression.

WHAT IS PHYSICAL ABUSE?

Many parents use physical discipline. Slapping children's hands and spanking them are common ways to punish children for misbehaving. Mild physical punishment is not considered physical abuse. *Physical abuse* involves severe acts, such as hitting a child with a closed fist or with some object, like a stick. Physically abused babies often are shaken, sometimes to the point of causing brain damage or death. Older children may be kicked or thrown across the room. In extreme cases, the child is tortured or the parent puts the child's life at risk by choking or stabbing her. For most children, these are not everyday occurrences. Physical abuse tends to happen now and then; between times, the child may have an adequate relationship with the parent, although often these parents are critical and easily annoyed even when they are not being physically abusive. In many ways, it is useful to think of physical abuse as an extreme form of parental rejection, as I discussed in chapter 5.

Physically abused children often live in families where violence is used to solve problems. The parent who abuses the child may also abuse a spouse, or both spouses may abuse each other. In these families, children learn it is acceptable to get your own way by bullying and hurting people who are smaller or weaker. Professionals who work with maltreated children believe that just being exposed to family violence can be as damaging to children as being physically abused.

WHAT IS NEGLECT?

Parents who seem disinterested in the parental role are said to be *neglectful*. Neglectful parents do not meet their children's physical and/or emotional needs, and they seem disinterested in the child's development as a person. Neglect is an extreme form of parental indifference, as I described in chapter 5. It is the most common form of child maltreatment. However, it is harder to define than physical abuse because it involves the absence of good parenting, while physical abuse involves clearly inappropriate parenting. Because neglect is so hard to define, it can be difficult for adult women to recognize that they were neglected as children.

The most common form of neglect involves the child being left alone and unsupervised for long periods of time. The parent may go off to work in the morning and leave the child to make her own breakfast and lunch and get off to school. The child may not get enough good food to eat or she may watch TV for hours or go to the mall instead of going to school. In extreme cases, unmonitored children can end up in situations where they are hurt or sexually abused.

Neglectful parents often do not provide enough structure for their children in the form of a consistent and predictable routine. Children's emotional security depends in part on knowing what is going to happen. Neglected children may grow up in homes where the food runs out or no one comes home to take care of them. People may come and go from their lives with little explanation. From the child's point of view, her family may seem disorganized or even chaotic. For instance, one woman I worked with was often left waiting in the dark hallway after school because her mother had forgotten to pick her up.

Neglect tends to be an ongoing situation rather than one that happens from time to time, and for this reason it can be more harmful to children even than physical abuse.

PARENTS WHO MALTREAT

Together, physical abuse, neglect, and sexual abuse are called *child maltreatment*. Although professionals who work with abused children were originally interested in studying a particular form of maltreatment, over the years they've realized that most abused children experience more than one form of abuse. One common combination is neglect and sexual abuse, which occurs because the child is not adequately supervised. In addition, there are ways in which parents who maltreat are similar to one another regardless of how they maltreat. I have taken the following information on their similarities and differences from reviews of the research literature written by Black, Heyman, and Smith Slep (2001) and Wilson, Kuebli, and Hughes (2005).

Similarities

Many of the parents who maltreat were maltreated themselves during childhood. About a third of the parents who physically abuse their children were physically abused themselves. As adults, parents who maltreat still feel alienated from their own parents with whom they usually have little contact.

Parents who maltreat feel stressed and isolated. They have very few positive things to say about their children, who they see as a source of stress and conflict. They say they have no one to talk to, particularly about their struggles as parents. They can be easily upset and angered and have great difficulty controlling their negative emotions. They may be depressed or addicted to drugs or alcohol, which they use in an attempt to cope. Clearly, parents who maltreat their children are themselves hurt. A major goal of professionals in this area is to find a way to stop maltreated children from becoming maltreating parents.

Differences

There also are differences between parents who physically abuse or neglect their children. One of the biggest differences is that the vast majority of neglecting parents are young single mothers who are living in poverty. Most of the research on neglect is done with children who for some reason have come to the attention of government authorities. These children may have been removed from the home because of the neglect, or the family may be monitored by a government agency to ensure it does not happen again. Neglectful parents who are wealthy may be less likely to come to the attention of government authorities and less likely to lose their children than are poor parents. The wealthy parent who leaves his child alone at home while he spends the weekend at a ski resort may not come to the attention of authorities, but his child is just as neglected as the child of a single, poor parent.

In contrast, physical abuse cuts across social classes. Physical abuse may be more likely to come to the authorities' attention than neglect because it is more likely to leave physical evidence in the form of bruises and broken bones. This may be the reason that physical abuse is just as likely to be detected whether parents are wealthy or poor.

Physically abusive parents are more easily angered than neglectful parents. There is more conflict in their homes, and they are more likely to have grown up in a family where violence was used to solve problems. They often have unrealistic expectations for their children, and they react with anger and violence when their children fail to meet these expectations. In general, parents who are physically abusive are more likely to be authoritarian.

Lisa's father was authoritarian. In chapter 4, I described how he kicked her dog across the room when he was angry with her. He also used extreme forms of physical discipline that verged on maltreatment. Punishment was a ritualized affair that could take as long as an hour, each minute adding to Lisa's terror as she anticipated the pain. His approach to discipline was sadistic. He seemed to think that effective punishment meant causing Lisa as much physical pain and humiliation as possible. Lisa's father was a wealthy businessman who was highly regarded in his community. To my knowledge, no authority ever became aware of or tried to stop the physical abuse she experienced.

PHYSICAL ABUSE HURTS CHILDREN

Maltreated children are at high risk for social and emotional problems. The kinds of problems they experience depend on how they were mistreated. I have taken the following descriptions of maltreated children from reviews of the research literature written by Kaplan, Pelcovitz, and Labruna (1999) and Trickett and McBride-Chang (1995).

Physically abused children and those who witness violence in their families are angry from a very early age. They see the world as a dangerous place, and they quickly react with anger to any perceived threat. For instance, they often see other children's behavior as more aggressive than it really is. Young children often try to take toys from one another; a child who tries to take a toy away from a physically abused child may find himself being knocked over the head with it. As physically abused children get older, they don't wait for other children to be aggressive. They bully other children, both verbally and physically. As a result, children who come from violent homes are disliked and often rejected by other children. As teenagers, they may run away from home, and because they have no way to support themselves, they may turn to crime. Physically abused girls often get involved in romantic relationships with boys and men who hurt them; boys from violent homes often are violent in their own intimate relationships.

Children and adolescents who were physically abused or exposed to family violence often are depressed. However, their depression typically is not recognized. Parents and teachers see them as sarcastic and disobedient. Even the child may not realize that a thin layer of anger masks sadness and vulnerability. Women with this background are at high risk for committing suicide. They believe that violence—even violence directed at their own bodies—is an acceptable solution to their problems.

LISA: *A CREDIT CARD WRAPPED IN BLANK PAPER*

Lisa showed some characteristics of a physically abused child. Her anger took the form of suspicion. As a child, she did not believe anyone could be trusted to treat her with warmth and compassion, so she withdrew from all human relationships. Although she did not go out of her way to bully other children, she was cold and surly and deliberately pushed other children away by being mean to them.

As an adolescent, Lisa shoplifted. At the time, she did not know why she stole things she easily could have bought with her allowance, but as an adult she wondered if she was looking for a way to humiliate her father. In therapy, she recalled a time when she shoplifted from a department store. When she was caught by the security guards, she waited with relish for her father to come get her. As she hoped, her father was embarrassed, but because he was so well known in the community, he was able to get her out of the store without charges. He took her home and began the ritualized punishment she had endured since early childhood. Lisa remembered her defiance as she accepted the punishment. For the first time in her life, she did not cry or ask him to stop. She looked in his eyes and without being able to say why, she knew she had won. He never punished her again, and shortly after this incident she left home.

Lisa drifted into marriage with a man she also experienced as physically abusive. In this case, the physical abuse took the form of coercive, sadistic sex that left her feeling scared and humiliated. As had been the case with her father, she did not feel it was possible to stand up to David and tell him to stop.

When we first worked together, Lisa often talked about committing suicide. She kept a bottle of poison at home, carefully sealed so her children couldn't open it and mislabeled so David did not know what it was. There is no question Lisa was very depressed. However, it was not unbearable sadness that drove her to consider suicide. It was rage. She plotted her suicide down to the smallest detail. She knew how long the poison would take to work, and she planned to take it at a time that guaranteed she would die after her children were in bed. She planned to be discovered by David when he came home after working late or staying out with his friends. She would leave no note—only a blank piece of paper folded around the credit card she held in her married name. When she was angry with David, she would go over this plan in her mind, cherishing the details the way a child might fondle a beloved toy. Her suicide plan comforted her. She had learned from her father that she could triumph over her husband by destroying herself.

NEGLECT HURTS CHILDREN

The child who is physically abused acts out against the world in anger. The one who is neglected withdraws from it in resignation. As young children, neglected kids seem lonely and sad. They have no friends and seem to prefer playing alone. When they are stressed, they are quick to give up and claim that nothing they do will help. Even at this young age, they experience feelings of anxiety and depression.

When neglected children go to school, they carry a negative view of people with them. They stay on the edge of other children's activities, watching, or they avoid other children altogether. As a result, they are not accepted. They are not rejected in the same way physically abused children are; they are overlooked. One neglected child said she would rather stay inside during lunchtime recess and help the janitor clean up the cafeteria than risk approaching the children in the playground. Their social isolation puts neglected children at risk for sexual victimization by people outside the family. An adult who shows interest in them is like water to someone dying of thirst.

As adolescents, physically abused children are runaways; neglected children are throwaways. They may leave home because they feel it does not matter whether they stay or go. They can drift into crime, especially prostitution, to support themselves. As adults, they are at risk for anxiety and depression.

TRACY: *THE DIRTY LITTLE SECRET*

Tracy was a neglected child. Her parents drank heavily and often left their daughters alone and unsupervised. Even at an early age, Tracy did what a lot of older children in neglectful families do: she tried to be a mother to her younger sister, Cassie.

Tracy's parents separated, and she never saw her father again. For several years, her mother left Tracy and Cassie alone while she worked multiple jobs to support them. Her mother would leave early in the morning and not return until late at night, so Tracy did the laundry, groceries, and cooking, and she got Cassie and herself off to school. Although Tracy's mother told her children she was working, Tracy suspected her mother spent her evenings with men in bars. Sometimes the girls were left in the care of neighborhood boys who tried to touch them sexually. When Tracy told her mother, her mother accused her of exaggerating to get attention.

A number of men passed through their lives until Tracy's mother married Joe. He did not have a steady job, so the girls were left alone with him while their mother worked. Before long, he tried to molest them. Tracy would hit him or run away, and after awhile he left her alone. She did not bother telling her mother because her mother had not taken her seriously when she told her about the boys. Then Tracy learned Joe was sexually abusing Cassie. This time she did tell her mother. To her horror, her mother said she knew about the abuse but had decided not to do anything because she did not want to lose Joe. Tracy's mother blamed Cassie for dressing "sexy" and "flirting" with Joe. When Tracy tried to protect Cassie by involving the authorities, her mother convinced them Tracy was making up stories because she did not like her stepfather.

When I first worked with Tracy, she did not see what had happened to her as "neglect." As a child, she thought her life was normal. As a teenager, she was ashamed of her mother and she lied to cover up for her. However, for most of her adulthood she had stuck to the story that her mother was a hardworking woman who loved her daughters and did everything she could to support them. Adults who were neglected as children often find it extremely difficult to define their experiences as neglect.

A Dawning Awareness

From our first session, Tracy described her mother as "crazy." Tracy's grandmother had been hospitalized with mental illness for most of her adult life, and Tracy thought her mother had inherited her grandmother's "craziness."

As a child, Tracy quickly learned to turn down the volume when it came to her attachment needs. She lowered her expectations for her mother. She tried to figure out what her mother needed from her and to do that as well as possible. Primarily, her mother did not want any trouble from her daughters. Tracy did her best. She tried to reduce her mother's burden by taking over the household chores. Yet no matter how good Tracy tried to be, her mother told her she was "difficult" and "too much to handle."

Tracy's mother probably had not been parented well herself. She was a very young woman when she had Tracy, and she seems to have lacked the qualities needed to provide a stable home and to be a loving mother. She struggled with alcohol and probably with other emotional problems throughout Tracy's life.

Tracy's view of her mother was clarified by events that happened when we had worked together for only a short time. Cassie had struggled with emotional problems for many years as a result of her sexual abuse by Joe. She had been involved with countless men who had fathered her children but were no longer in her life. Tracy worried that Cassie was on the same path as their mother, and she felt great empathy for Cassie's children whose lives she saw unfolding as her own had done. So Tracy was thrilled when Cassie went back to school to become a hairdresser. Tracy hoped this was the beginning of a new life for Cassie.

Imagine Tracy's dismay when their mother brought Joe to Cassie's graduation. Tracy could not contain herself. She told her mother it was unacceptable to bring Joe given how badly he had messed up Cassie's life. She reminded her mother that Cassie herself had banned Joe from her home because she feared he would sexually abuse her children. Her mother defended Joe, saying that what he had done was in the past and should be forgiven.

Tracy told me she was astonished that her mother was "so selfish she [couldn't] see how she hurt other people." Tracy realized that only selfishness and lack of empathy could explain why her mother had allowed Joe to sexually abuse Cassie. Her mind was flooded with examples of her mother's selfishness. Now that she was a mother, she understood what hard work mothering is. In many ways, she said, it was easier to go to a job and leave your kids at home than it was to be a good parent. She told me she suspected for the first time that her mother had deliberately escaped her responsibilities to her children by spending so much time at work.

A Conversation About Attachment

In our next session, Tracy told me she felt as if a burden had been lifted from her shoulders. At first, she had doubted what she had remembered of her childhood. She didn't want to "tell [me] lies," so she had asked a friend who knew her as a child. The friend confirmed that Tracy's mom was a "pathetic" parent. Tracy had decided to talk to her mother. She said she wanted two things from their conversation: she wanted her mother to admit that she had neglected her daughters, and she wanted to know what her mother was thinking and feeling at the time. She wanted to know why her mother had made the choices she had.

Clients often want to have this kind of conversation once they realize what they experienced as children. I think of it as a conversation about attachment. It's important for the client to hear that her parent was not available and responsive to her needs when she was a child. All their lives, insecurely attached children have heard that they are the ones who have the problem. The parent tells them that the way he or she treats them is fine and that they are too sensitive and too demanding. As adults, clients need to hear that what they experienced was real, and that the parent knows he or she let them down. They need the parent to validate their experience.

Tracy also needed to hear her mother's perspective. As the Oscar Wilde quote at the beginning of this chapter observes, children start out loving their parents. They may pass through a period of judging them, but ultimately they want to love them again. In order to love them, children have to be able to forgive, and to forgive they must understand why the parent made the choices she did. A conversation about attachment is not only an opportunity to heal the rift between a parent and an insecurely attached child. It also is an opportunity to establish a new attachment relationship to take them into the future.

Unfortunately, Tracy's mother was not up to the task of having this conversation. Sometimes parents aren't. She told Tracy that since she had not been sexually abused like her sister, she had no right to complain about how she had been treated.

The Dirty Little Secret

To her credit, Tracy did the work of the conversation without her mother. Before their conversation, she had always felt there must be something wrong with her that had caused her mother to treat her as she did. She had always assumed that she had deserved to be treated badly for being a difficult child. When her mother told her that only Cassie had grounds for complaint, Tracy realized that her mother was not capable of being a good parent. She told me that normal mothers do not leave their children alone and uncared for. Most of the behavior that Tracy's mother had labeled "difficult" was normal stuff like experimenting with cigarettes. Now Tracy could see that her mother's neglect had nothing to do with her and everything to do with her mother's lack of preparation and perhaps even her unwillingness to be a mother. Tracy said she felt good about understanding her childhood in this way. She felt that seeing her mother's inadequacies made her "stronger but softer instead of bitter."

Tracy described her childhood neglect as her family's "dirty little secret." She explained that everyone in the family pretended they had had a normal family and that their mother had worked hard to support them. Now Tracy saw that her mother had been ill prepared and perhaps unwilling to be a mother and that she had stayed away from home to avoid her responsibilities as a parent. The neglect Tracy experienced as a child had been her blind spot.

WHY MALTREATMENT LEADS TO DEPRESSION

All forms of childhood maltreatment put women at risk for depression. However, neglect and childhood sexual abuse are particularly strong factors in adult depression. Why does maltreatment put women at risk?

Neurobiology

At the most basic level, trauma during childhood, including neglect and physical and sexual abuse, can cause permanent changes to the nervous system that make people highly reactive to stress (Van Voorhees and Scarpa 2004). They react more strongly to lower levels of stress than do people without trauma in their past. In addition, their biological response to stress lasts longer. Situations that were very negative and over which the child had little control are especially likely to lead to these neurobiological changes.

Women with a history of maltreatment may be biologically prepared to react more intensely to stress. They could benefit from antidepressant medication such as Prozac when they find themselves in stressful circumstances. Although this idea makes sense in theory, little research has been done on it. Yet many women with this kind of background are prescribed Prozac as a "preventive" measure.

Stress and Coping

Women with a history of childhood maltreatment experience stressful events more often than do other women (Kessler 1997). In particular, they experience more instances of stress in close relationships. Thus, in part, women with a history of maltreatment may be at risk for depression because they experience more interpersonal stress. The more stress women experience, the more likely they are to become depressed.

In addition, there are differences in the ways that women with and without a maltreatment history cope with stress (Leitenberg, Gibson, and Novy 2004). Women who were maltreated as children cope by avoiding or ignoring their problems, which can lead to depression. They also are unlikely to believe that other people will be available and responsive to their emotional needs because this is not what they learned as children in their families. What they learned was that they have to take care of themselves, that others will not be there for them, and perhaps that others do not even care about their distress.

Attachment Insecurity

Attachment insecurity is the norm among children with a history of maltreatment. Neglected children can show either of the insecure attachment patterns. However, because parental neglect is an extreme form of indifference, these children are somewhat more likely to respond by turning down the volume.

Physically abused children tend to be *disorganized* with regard to their attachment needs (Cassidy and Mohr 2001). This means they do not consistently use either of the strategies I discussed previously. At times, they are angry and demand reassurance, while at other times they run away or avoid closeness in relationships. Disorganized attachment is seen primarily among children who have experienced physical or sexual abuse. It's not surprising that abused kids are confused: the person who can comfort them is also the person who hurts them.

If a maltreated child can establish a secure relationship with an adult in a caregiving role, like a relative or a teacher, she will be at lower risk for depression when she is an adult. Only children who are both maltreated and insecurely attached are at increased risk (Toth and Cicchetti 1996). However, the chances of finding another person to whom a secure attachment can be formed are low. In part, this is because maltreated children generalize from the relationship with the maltreating parent to other adults. Children who have not been maltreated usually show a range of attachment strategies with different people. For instance, a child could be securely attached to her parents but insecurely attached to her critical and demanding teacher. Children usually discriminate among the people who look after them, and they form secure or insecure attachments based on the real qualities of each relationship. However, maltreated children are much more likely to show the same insecure strategy in all of their relationships, possibly because they expect other adults to treat them the same way their maltreating parent did.

TRACY: *THE PAST BECOMES THE PRESENT*

For Tracy, turning down the volume was adaptive as long as she lived with her mother. During Tracy's childhood, her mother had shown repeatedly that she could not be counted on to care for and protect Tracy. Tracy lowered her expectations of her mother. However, in important ways, Tracy's response was not typical of a neglected child. Rather than withdrawing from life and other people, she met life head-on. She responded to her early childhood experiences by becoming a problem solver. She was self-reliant, but she also cared for other people, especially Cassie.

For the most part, solving problems worked well for Tracy. She got herself through university and into a good job where she earned enough money to provide for her mother and sister. Sometimes she had to make sacrifices that they neither acknowledged nor seemed to appreciate, which hurt Tracy's feelings. And sometimes she felt guilty about Cassie's sexual abuse. She blamed herself for not doing enough to protect her sister. When we accept responsibility for others, we also take on the blame when things go wrong. However, these were small discomforts. Importantly, Tracy never felt depressed during her childhood and adolescence. As long as she could solve problems, she felt strong and capable.

In Matt, Tracy chose a partner who was used to being looked after. In his late twenties he still lived at home. His mother took care of all his needs. He couldn't cook or operate a washing machine.

A woman who was used to both giving and receiving care in her relationships might have taken one look at Matt and passed, but not Tracy. Her experience within her family had taught her to look after people; she simply added Matt to her list. Tracy had more than turned down the volume; she had turned it right off. It never occurred to her that someday she might need to be taken care of herself.

Tracy's relationship with Matt worked as long as she did not need his help. He made few demands on her, either materially or emotionally, which suited Tracy because she was still very involved with her mother and sister. Most importantly, Tracy could stay in control. Matt left all the decisions to her and never argued with the outcome. For Tracy, their relationship was ideal. She had someone fun to hang out with who let her have things exactly the way she wanted.

Everything changed when their son Michael was born. Suddenly Tracy felt overwhelmed by her responsibilities. She had had enough people to look after with her mother, sister, and Matt; adding a baby to the list put her over the top. Worse, when she looked around for help, she realized she had no one to turn to. Although she had looked after Cassie's children many times, Cassie never volunteered to take Michael for a few hours so Tracy could get a break. Leaving him with her mother was out of the question, even if her mother had volunteered, which she did not. Matt disappeared into work.

Tracy knew she needed help. One time she tried to turn to Matt's mother, but she was surprised to learn that she was too "embarrassed" to ask for help. She had never asked anyone for help, and she didn't know how to do it without feeling weak.

In our sessions, Tracy began to examine each relationship, and she was dismayed to find the same pattern everywhere. Over the years, she had given money to her family and friends; she had listened to their troubles and provided advice; she had bought gifts for their birthdays and their children's birthdays; she had put them up when they needed a place to stay. She had done all this for them, yet now that she needed help, everyone was too busy.

As Tracy realized that she felt exploited in her relationships, she became sad. Not depressed, but genuinely sad that she seemed to have no friends or family who could be counted on. "What about Matt?" I asked. He seemed the obvious one to help. After all, Michael was his baby too. With great sad eyes, Tracy told me she had never believed she could count on Matt. "If your own family doesn't care about you," she explained, "why would anyone else?"

Questions to Ask Yourself

1. When I was a child, was I afraid of my parents? At times, did they get extremely angry with me? Did they sometimes hit me too hard? Did people in my family use physical force or anger to get their own way?

2. What impact did my parents' anger have on me? Was I an angry kid? Did I bully other kids? Was I sometimes mean to other kids for no good reason? Did I get involved with boys and men who treated me badly? Have I sometimes been so angry that I thought about committing suicide to get back at the people who've hurt me?

3. When I was child, did I feel like my parents didn't really care about me? Were they sometimes too busy to make sure I ate properly or went to school? Could I pretty much do what I wanted without worrying about them? Can I think of a time that I was left alone somewhere because they forgot all about me? If I needed them, were they there?

4. What impact did my parents' lack of care have on me? Was I sad or lonely as a kid? Did the other kids ignore me? Did I get involved with boys and men who ignored my needs?

5. Do I feel lonely? Do I feel as if no one really knows me or cares what happens to me?

CHAPTER 7

families that hurt: childhood sexual abuse

Girls and women are more likely than boys and men to be victims of violence. They are more likely to be beaten, sexually assaulted, or murdered, particularly by people who are intimately related to them: parents, children, romantic partners, and spouses. All types of interpersonal violence, including sexual and physical assault, are associated with depression, particularly for girls and women. The overwhelming majority of women who are seen at sexual-assault centers after being raped or at women's shelters after being assaulted by their partners are depressed. Depression after an assault can last for months or even years if the woman was victimized previously or the victimization continues.

In this chapter I focus on a particular type of victimization: sexual abuse during childhood. There is a very strong link between being sexually abused as a child and becoming depressed as an adult. One study looked at rates of sexual abuse among more than a hundred women who were seeking treatment for depression at a large general hospital (Murrey et al. 1993). Almost half of these women had been sexually abused as children. Women who have experienced many episodes of depression are especially likely to have a sexual abuse history (Andrews 1995). Sexual abuse may be one of the major reasons women experience more depression than men (Whiffen and Clark 1997).

Most of the women in the hospital study were not seeking help because of their sexual abuse. In fact, many women are unaware of the impact that childhood sexual abuse has on how they feel. Some women remember the abuse, but they don't connect it to why they feel depressed. They look for more immediate reasons, such as a recent loss or their marital or financial problems. Other women only have vague memories of the abuse. These women probably have never considered the possibility that what they have almost forgotten might make them depressed. Yet, as I will show in this chapter, talking about the sexual abuse can stop the revolving door of depression.

EVERYTHING OLD IS NEW AGAIN

In 1896, Sigmund Freud was a young, up-and-coming clinician and researcher in the emerging field of psychiatry when he published a scientific report, with his colleague Josef Breuer, entitled *Studies on Hysteria* (Breuer and Freud 1962). *Hysteria* was the most common psychiatric disorder that young women of his day suffered. In this book, Freud described the cases of eighteen women he had treated in his private practice. He claimed that during the course of treatment, the memory of childhood sexual abuse emerged for every one.

Initially, the women did not remember the abuse. Then they began to tell him what they remembered without any apparent understanding of what the memories meant. Gradually, strong feelings of anger, disgust, helplessness, and betrayal emerged. Throughout this process, the patients struggled against what they remembered. They expressed shock and disbelief. The women's attempts to discount what they remembered convinced Freud that what he was hearing were real memories. Freud said sexual abuse could explain why women are more prone to all kinds of emotional problems.

In a book called *The Assault on Truth*, Jeffrey Masson (1984) described the reaction of the scientific community to Freud's ideas: they were dismissed out of hand. After all, this was nineteenth-century Vienna, which, like most of Europe during that period, was not a place where sexuality was openly discussed. Freud began to doubt himself. To explain the high rates of hysteria in Europe at that time, a large number of children would have to have been abused. He wondered if he had made a mistake.

Although Freud never gathered any evidence that the memories of his patients were false, he eventually concluded they must be fantasies produced by the child's imagination. With a uniquely Freudian sleight of hand, he suggested that the memories were actually unfulfilled fantasies and wishes that the child used to cover up sexual feelings for the parent.

Officially, Freud took back his ideas about sexual abuse in 1905. However, the evidence linking sexual abuse to emotional distress is so compelling that it has resurfaced time and time again in the past hundred years. Independently, a French psychiatrist named Pierre Janet reached a similar conclusion (Janet 1907). He focused on *trauma* rather than sexual abuse specifically. A traumatic event is one that is shocking, terrifying, and overwhelming to the person who experiences it and which poses a threat to that person's safety. All forms of interpersonal victimization have the potential to be traumatic, including physical abuse and neglect.

Was Freud Right?

Large surveys of randomly selected households in the United States show that one in five girls and one in ten to twenty boys are sexually abused before the age of sixteen (Alpert, Brown, and Courtois 1998). Sexual abuse is defined in these surveys as unwanted sexual contact with someone at least five years older than the child. Freud was correct when he observed that childhood sexual abuse is pervasive.

THE SYMPTOMS OF SEXUAL ABUSE

Freud's description of the symptoms shown by women with a sexual abuse history also holds true. Generally, these women are less happy and more emotionally distressed than other women. While not all women will experience clinically significant problems, their risk is greater. In particular, women who were sexually abused as children are more likely to suffer from clinical depression and anxiety.

Women with an abuse history may show symptoms of a specific anxiety disorder, *post-traumatic stress disorder* (PTSD). People with PTSD experience two distinctive feeling states. In one state they are extremely fearful. They are bombarded by thoughts, waking visions, and vivid nightmares about the event that traumatized them. In the other state, they feel numb and disconnected from the world. They avoid thinking about the traumatic event, or they may even have amnesia for it. While some people with PTSD alternate between these states, others live for years in the numb and disconnected state.

Amnesia for a traumatic event is a form of *dissociation*. Dissociation is believed to be a normal attempt to protect ourselves from overwhelming events, either by forgetting them or by distancing ourselves from them so they don't seem real, which lessens their emotional impact. For example, people who have been in car accidents often say they felt as though they were moving in slow motion or watching themselves in a movie, both of which are forms of dissociation. People are believed to use dissociation to maintain the numb and disconnected state of PTSD.

An extreme form of dissociation involves women experiencing their identity as fragmented into different parts. This is called *dissociative identity disorder* (DID). Women who have endured severe, repeated, and sadistic abuse can experience themselves as having many different parts or identities. The traumatic memory is given over to one or more parts of the self and forgotten unless these parts of the self are evoked.

Many women with an abuse history report dissociative experiences. For instance, they can have out-of-body experiences during painful events like childbirth. When children are sexually abused, they may develop the ability to feel as if they are leaving their bodies as a way of coping with the abuse. These women also may experience strange sensations that don't seem to have a medical explanation, like unexplained pain. Later they may learn that the sensation relates directly to the abuse. For instance, a woman who was forced to perform oral sex as a child had a feeling of choking as an adult. Sometimes these sensations are called *body memories* because they seem to be the body's memory of specific abuse events.

RECALLING THE ABUSE

Freud's description of the process by which abuse is recalled also continues to be true. When women start therapy, they may seem to have forgotten the abuse altogether or they may have memories but fail to understand what the memories mean. As therapy continues, they may go through a period of denial. They may even quit therapy for a time because they do not want to believe that the abuse happened. It is very important that a woman not feel pushed by her therapist to prematurely accept or reject what she seems to remember. She must come to her own decision about the "truth." Eventually, the weight of the evidence leads many women to accept what they remember, and they are able to move on to the phase of *reprocessing*. In this phase, the client and therapist try to get a picture of what happened to the client and how these events have had an impact on how she feels about herself and her adult relationships. They try to reorganize her understanding of herself and others in light of the abuse she experienced.

TRUE OR FALSE

Freud struggled with whether to believe what his patients remembered; contemporary clinicians face the same dilemma. Establishing the objective "truth" of an abuse memory is difficult and can be impossible unless another person who was in the position to know the truth, like a sibling or parent, admits the abuse occurred. Most people trust their memories. However, psychologists know that memories are unreliable.

The problem stems from the fact that the abuse occurred to a child. Very few people have continuous memory for the events that occurred to them before the age of about six. Most people have only isolated memories of particularly happy or sad events. No one is sure why memory is incomplete in the preschool years, but it is such a universal experience that there is probably a biological explanation.

Children can form incomplete or even erroneous memories of events that happened earlier in their lives. My son swears that when he was about two years old, he dropped a Chicken Nugget between the rails of our deck and cried inconsolably. Because I was there, I know that this memory combines two separate lunches on our deck: one where he dropped a Chicken Nugget but shrugged and carried on eating and one where he cried because the food was hot and burned his mouth. However, I can't convince him that what he remembers never happened. Memories that are false can seem as real as memories that are true.

The False-Memory Debate

Elizabeth Loftus is a psychologist and a distinguished memory researcher. Her early research showed that what people remember when they witness traffic accidents or crime is often inaccurate. In 1992, she began a series of studies which showed that *false memories* can be created in the lab (Loftus 2001). A false memory is exactly what it sounds like—an apparent memory for something that never happened. One famous Loftus study involved convincing people they had been lost in a mall as children. None of the participants actually had been lost, but the more detail they were given about the alleged event and the more they trusted the source (for instance, if a sibling told them the story), the more likely they were to believe it had happened. Most important, they actually claimed to remember the event, even though it had never happened.

At the time Loftus started this research, it was not uncommon for therapists to suggest to clients that they might have been sexually abused as children. Clients were encouraged to do exercises to "help them remember," including writing about their childhood, and drawing or imagining childhood events. Unfortunately, the simple act of imagining an event makes it seem more real. On the basis of her research, Loftus argued that any "memories" that resulted from these kinds of suggestions should be viewed with suspicion. She was most concerned about women who had no memory of abuse prior to the beginning of therapy.

Some lawyers and alleged abusers took Loftus's research to mean that all memories of sexual abuse are unreliable. Until that time, judges and juries had accepted the testimony of adult women who claimed to have been sexually abused as children; now their testimony was brought into question. In response, other researchers began to conduct studies to evaluate various aspects of Loftus's argument. This research was reviewed for the American Psychological Association by Alpert, Brown, and Courtois (1998).

The first type of study tried to find out how common it is for sexual abuse to be forgotten during some later period of life. In three studies, women were interviewed years after their childhood abuse was documented by contact with the authorities. Although the majority of women had at least partial memory for the abuse throughout their lives, a significant minority, up to 40 percent, had a period during which they did not remember the abuse. Forgetting was more likely when the abuse had occurred earlier in childhood.

Other studies asked women what triggers caused them to recall the abuse after a period of either partial or total forgetting. The most commonly named triggers were reading or hearing about sexual abuse in the media, experiencing something similar to the original abuse, or having a sexual experience. Less than 15 percent of women said they remembered sexual abuse as the result of being in therapy. In fact, many women seek psychotherapy because they are beginning to remember the abuse.

Why Children Forget

There are at least two possible reasons why traumatic events like sexual abuse may be incompletely remembered or even totally forgotten for periods of time. The first is that traumatic events are less likely to be remembered in words and more likely to be remembered as physical sensations. Children, in particular, often act out the abuse even though they cannot say what happened to them (Burgess, Hartman, and Baker 1995). Another possibility is that partial or total forgetting is due to dissociation. Interestingly, children are much more likely than adults to dissociate during and after a traumatic event (Alpert, Brown, and Courtois 1998).

The Middle Ground

Today most clinicians have found a middle ground between the old practice of dismissing reports of childhood sexual abuse as "unfulfilled fantasies" and the practice in the early 1990s of treating these memories as if they were absolutely true. Loftus's research was a wake-up call to therapists to avoid imposing their theories on their clients. Both clients and therapists need to live with the possibility that they will never know what "really happened." And in the end, it is the client who must decide how to understand her past in a way that allows her to move beyond it.

LISA: *HER EARLY SESSIONS*

From my first session with Lisa, I was aware of the possibility that she had been sexually abused. She said she felt "debased" in her sexual relationship with her husband. At the same time, she said her only value came from being a sex object. It is unusual for marital problems to focus so specifically on sex. In our first session I learned that her sister and David had had an affair. Lisa didn't seem to think it was unusual that this affair involved a relative. In families where sexual abuse has occurred, normal sexual taboos often are missing.

After only a few sessions, Lisa revealed she had been sexually abused by her uncle—her father's brother—between the ages of nine and twelve. However, she did not think about what had happened to her as "abuse." She described it as an "affair." I asked if she had told anyone about the "affair," and she said that as a child she had told her mother, who asked Lisa to go along with her uncle because he was a bachelor who "needed a sexual outlet."

The adult way Lisa talked about the abuse by her uncle made me wonder if she hadn't been abused at a younger age. Her mother's encouragement made me wonder if her father was the original abuser. My suspicions were heightened when Lisa described a panic attack she had while making love. She told me she experienced the feeling of a crushing weight on her chest. When I asked what the weight reminded her of, she said matter-of-factly, "My father." However, she couldn't or wouldn't explain her comment further.

Although the picture Lisa painted of her childhood clearly pointed in the direction of sexual abuse by her father, she was unaware of this possibility at the beginning of therapy and she struggled against believing it for several months. It was as if she knew but didn't know at the same time. It was only when her father suggested she engage in sexual acts with her son that Lisa began to seriously consider the possibility that he had sexually abused her.

At about the same time, she had a fight with her husband, David. She accused him of flirting with another woman at a party. In defending himself, he told her "you must have imagined it," a phrase that brought on a flood of memories suggestive of childhood attempts to tell someone what was happening to her. She remembered she had been withdrawn from her art class "because of something [she] drew." She remembered a meeting with a teacher during which her parents had repeatedly assured the teacher that Lisa had a "vivid imagination."

Then the abuse memories started. They could be triggered by anything, especially by the senses of smell, touch, and sound. One spring day she cleaned out the closet in her hallway. The smell of wool coats and damp mittens triggered a memory of being abused by her father on a pile of winter coats. Other memories began as repetitive physical gestures. The feel of her son's eraser in her palm evolved over a couple of days into a repetitive gesture of squeezing and releasing, which she gradually identified as manually stimulating her father's penis. It was as if her body remembered incidents that her mind had forgotten.

Lisa didn't trust her new memories. She said they must have been dreams or fantasies from childhood, an idea she got from listening to a psychiatrist on a radio talk show. She blamed herself for the images in her mind, telling me she must be sick to imagine such things. However, saying the images weren't real didn't stop them.

If I Forget the Past, I Lose an Eye

The Australian Aborigines have a saying: if I forget the past, I lose an eye. Without a clear picture of our past, we cannot fully see the present. Lisa took this saying one step further. As she told me when she began remembering the abuse by her father, "If I want to stop feeling depressed, I have to open my eyes." She understood that when we don't see ourselves and our past accurately, we are at risk for depression. Lisa's blind spot was the sexual abuse by her father that she experienced during childhood.

WHY SEXUAL ABUSE LEADS TO DEPRESSION

Sexual abuse has an impact on how children react to and cope with stress, on the way they feel about themselves, and on their relationships.

Stress and Coping

As I discussed in chapters 2 and 6, children who experience trauma of all kinds may be biologically primed to react strongly to stress. In addition, women with an abuse history often cope with stress in ways that are ineffective. They cope by avoiding or ignoring the problem, particularly when they are trying to deal with the painful feelings created by their childhood experiences. Remember that women are more likely to avoid or ignore problems that they feel they have no control over. For many women, the sexual abuse happened years ago. They may feel there is nothing they can do about it but temporarily reduce the bad feelings they frequently have. However, avoiding and ignoring the abuse puts them at risk for depression (Runtz and Schallow 1997).

Ignoring painful feelings may have been adaptive at the time the abuse was happening; an abused child really does lack control over the abuse. However, continuing to avoid bad feelings as an adult can lead women to stay in new painful situations, such as an unhappy marriage. Lisa had many warning signs that her marriage was in trouble before David told her about his illegitimate child. Because she ignored these warning signs, the marriage got worse until she could no longer deny it was in trouble.

SELF-SOOTHING

An important part of therapy for these women involves learning how to self-soothe when they feel stressed. Self-soothing can be as simple as taking a bath, getting a massage, or going for a run—anything that calms the person down. Once a woman has calmed down, she is better able to think about her problems. Therapy also shows women how to think about problems in constructive ways. With a therapist's help, problems can be broken down into manageable pieces, feelings can be identified and sorted through, and possible solutions can be generated. Good therapy not only helps a woman solve her problems but also teaches her how to solve them for herself.

TURNING TO OTHERS

The protective effect of relationships is even greater for women with a history of sexual abuse than it is for other women (Whiffen, Judd, and Aube 1999). However, these women are at a disadvantage here too because they have many problems with relationships (Rumstein-McKean and Hunsley 2001). They find it harder to get close to and trust other people. They are less satisfied with their current romantic relationships or marriages, and they feel insecurely attached in them. They have more sexual problems. Women with an abuse history are more likely to be physically or sexually assaulted by their romantic partners. As a result, they are less likely to marry and more likely to divorce. For some women, relationships are so painful that they avoid them altogether.

It's understandable that a woman who was abused as a child would have difficulty being close to people. The abuse happened in the context of a relationship, typically one where a degree of safety and trust developed first. Children who are abused learn that other people cannot be counted on to protect and help them and that other people don't care when they hurt. We carry forward the things we learn about people early in our lives. So children who grow up with abuse may expect other people to abuse them too. As a result, they never really trust or get close to others.

Because they often feel stressed, they may interact with others in ways that are seen as angry and demanding, which pushes people away. In therapy, women with an abuse history learn how to find and keep good relationships. They learn to ask for comfort and support in ways that draw people toward them rather than pushing them away. Expressing vulnerable feelings, like hurt and sadness, is more likely to draw people toward you, but doing so feels dangerous unless you trust that this person will not exploit your vulnerability. For some women, the therapist is the first person they learn to trust.

Much of the work Lisa did in therapy involved trust. Later in this chapter, I talk about the problems she had trusting me. We also did a lot of work to improve her relationship with David. He was devastated when she told him early in therapy that she wanted to leave him. He promised to change and offered to go to couple therapy. In individual therapy, I worked with Lisa to get her to express her thoughts, feelings, and needs to David and to tell him when she felt debased or abused by their sexual relations. Once he got over the shock of learning that his father-in-law, a man he liked and admired, had sexually abused Lisa, he was able to respond to his wife's needs. Most important, David was able to let her be angry with him, even though her anger did not always make sense to him. Once Lisa understood the impact of the abuse and was able to better manage her feelings, she and David went for couple therapy. They needed only a half-dozen sessions with a therapist who knew about Lisa's background and was experienced in working with couples to make a dramatic difference to their marriage.

The Defective Self

A central feeling in depression is shame. The shame-filled person feels at their core that they are not good enough. They don't deserve to be treated well, to be loved or admired, to be successful or praised. A shame-filled person feels in their heart that they do not deserve to have anything good happen to them because they are bad. Conversely, anything bad that happens must be their fault. While people who are not prone to depression take credit for their successes and blame their failures on external factors, the depressed person does the opposite.

Shame is an emotion associated with being a victim. People experience shame when they have been dominated, controlled, and defeated by another person—a bully, a controlling parent, or an adult who sexually or physically abused them. So it's not surprising that women who were abused as children feel more shame than other women do.

Often this shame is focused on their bodies (Andrews 1995). They may experience shame about a particular area of the body, such as the breasts, buttocks, or genitals, and they may go to great lengths to cover up this part. Maybe they undress in the closet when their husband is present or can't make love in the daytime. They may wear oversized clothes to disguise their figures or gain weight so they are unattractive to men.

It makes sense that sexually abused children feel shame. In many cultures, sexuality is shameful. The abuser also usually blames the child for the abuse. Abusers tell children they were sexually provocative and made the abuser have erotic feelings for them. They tell children that sexual acts are shameful and should be hidden from other people. Of course, they say these things because they don't want to take responsibility for the abuse and because they don't want to be caught. However, the child is unable to see the adult's real motivations. In the child's mind, something terrible is happening and it is her fault. The tendency to blame herself for uncontrollable, negative events may become a part of the abused child's personality such that she believes that even life events that are clearly out of her control are her fault.

Some factors increase the likelihood that an abused child will feel shame. When the abuse occurs over a long period of time and/or when it involves intercourse, the child is more likely to feel shame (Coffey et al. 1996). Another factor that creates shame is the reaction of other people. If others find out about the abuse and express disgust, shock, or disbelief, the child is more likely to feel shame.

The research on shame may explain why girls are more prone to depression after puberty—an age when they first become aware of their sexuality. Girls who were sexually abused at an earlier age may be ambivalent about normal, physical changes that make them interested in having sexual relationships. Their own sexual feelings may reawaken feelings of shame that were connected with the abuse.

A woman who feels shame expects other people to reject her and/or to be scornful of her supposed defects. This expectation comes directly from her belief that she is defective and unworthy. Women with an abuse history are always on the lookout for signs they will be rejected or put down. Sadly, when we look for rejection, we usually can find it, because human relationships are complicated and open to interpretation. As adults, these women may feel rejected or put down in response to both real and imagined maltreatment. Expectations can lead women with an abuse history to isolate themselves to prevent further humiliation or to attack others before they are attacked. Shame may keep women from developing the very relationships that could be used to soothe their distress and make them feel better about themselves.

LISA: *DISGUST TURNS TO SHAME*

When Lisa first remembered the abuse by her father, she was plagued by constant nausea. She said it was like the first few months of pregnancy. She couldn't keep any food down. Overwhelmed by weakness, she would lie on the couch in her living room with a bucket by her side. From time to time, she would retch. She was literally disgusted by what she remembered.

As she accepted what had happened to her, the nausea gave way to intense shame. The disgust was turned toward herself. Once she remembered the abuse, she also remembered being sexually aroused by the things her father did to her. She described becoming a compulsive masturbator as a child to please her father. She would practice so she could have more frequent and more intense orgasms. She confessed that the abuse by her uncle was not traumatic at the time it happened, and that, as an adult, she had once engaged in consensual sex with him. These revelations were the source of unbearable shame for Lisa. She worried that she deserved to be abused and that she invited sexual contact as a way of getting attention from men.

It took many months to soften her self-blame. I listened nonjudgmentally to the stories she told. When I did comment, I put the responsibility onto the father and uncle, and I talked about the lengths to which children will go to gain approval, especially in a family atmosphere of disapproval, fear, and criticism.

Two external events helped Lisa to develop sympathy for the child she had been. First, she began attending a group for sexual abuse survivors where she discovered that all of the women lived with shame. Listening to their stories, she felt compassion for the children they had been. As she realized they were not to blame for what adults had done to them, she was able to forgive herself. The second event was that she learned her younger sister also had been abused by their father. Lisa remembered her younger sister as a child. She remembered how innocent she had been. She was able to see that they both had been innocent children, used by their father.

Family Context

Typically, children who are abused do not grow up in happy, healthy families. The families of abused children often are filled with conflict and violence. The sexual abuse may be part of a bigger picture in which family members are dominated and coerced, physically or emotionally. As I described in chapter 4, Lisa's family was of this type.

Another type of family that puts children at risk for sexual abuse is one in which they are neglected. As I discussed in chapter 6, Tracy's family was of this kind, and she and her sister were both put at risk for sexual abuse as a result. Children from neglecting families are more likely to be victimized, and if they talk about what is happening to them, they are less likely to be helped. Women with a sexual abuse history who feel they were not loved or cared for by their parents during childhood are at the greatest risk for depression (Wind and Silvern 1994).

WHAT TO EXPECT IF YOU SEEK THERAPY

Events that remind women of the sexual abuse can trigger memories and prompt them to seek therapy. One common trigger is the birth of a child. Sometimes the experience of childbirth triggers memories of being physically dominated and hurt. One woman I treated was fine after the birth of her first child—a son—but came for therapy after the birth of her daughter. Having a daughter made her keenly aware of the victimization that girls are more likely than boys to experience. Another trigger is having a child who reaches the age that the mother was when she was abused. Sometimes comparable situations, like being forced to have sex, will bring women into therapy.

I highly recommend that women with a sexual abuse history seek individual therapy. As Lisa's experience shows, both group and couple therapy can be helpful too. However, women do not get the maximum benefit from these types of therapy until they have done individual work. Depressed women who were sexually abused will benefit most from therapy that focuses on softening their feelings of shame and guilt; strengthening their relationships with friends, family, and romantic partners; and solving problems, especially interpersonal ones. Because children who are abused typically come from families with many other problems, you can expect to work on family issues as well as the abuse.

Individual therapy takes a long time. In my experience, a depressed woman with an abuse history will need about fifty sessions of individual therapy to become well. The more complicated the abuse—for example, by multiple abusers—and the more severe the depression, the greater the number of sessions that are needed. Lisa had almost sixty sessions of individual therapy spread out over an eighteen-month period.

One of the reasons therapy takes so long is that many women with an abuse history have never had a trusting relationship. In attachment theory terms, most have either turned down the volume or are *disorganized* in attachment relationships, which means that they sometimes turn the volume up and sometimes turn it down. Either strategy creates problems in therapy. What is common to the strategies is that the therapist is seen as untrustworthy. However, the response to the therapist differs greatly depending on which attachment strategy the client uses.

Women who turn down the volume may be easily angered by the therapist and may quit therapy prematurely. One woman quit therapy when I was unable to reschedule her session that day to accommodate a medical appointment. In contrast, women who are disorganized may feel both intensely needy and intensely angry with the therapist, and sessions may be taken over by a constant focus on their relationship. These women need to feel that the therapist is emotionally available to them but also that she sets reasonable limits. For example, the client cannot express her anger with the therapist in abusive ways.

Women with a sexual abuse history may not be aware that they don't trust others until they are in a situation where they are telling another person about events in their lives about which they feel deeply ashamed. Therapists who have experience working with these women take care to establish a good working relationship before they try to deal with the abuse. Throughout the therapy, they show respect for the client and they give her a great deal of control over the process. If a woman does not feel comfortable talking about the abuse or if she feels overwhelmed in a session, a good therapist will not push her.

As is the case with most therapy, it's a good idea to find a therapist who is experienced. However, previous experience with sexual abuse is not essential. Lisa was the first client I worked with who had been sexually abused, yet she made some of the biggest gains I have ever seen in therapy. General knowledge about the consequences of sexual abuse is critical. Women should feel comfortable asking potential therapists what they know about sexual abuse and its treatment.

The most important thing to pay attention to with a therapist is how you feel about him or her. If you feel you can trust this person and that they make sense and help you feel better, you are on the right track. However, it's always a good idea to give the therapist a second chance if you feel hurt or upset. Misunderstandings are inevitable between people. If the therapist says or does something you don't like, you need to tell her how you feel and give her a chance to explain or change her behavior.

Several years ago I was training a student to do therapy with sexually abused women. She had no personal experience with sexual abuse, and she was sometimes clumsy with her clients. Once she described a client as "having sex" with her father. The client was extremely upset and left the session without saying a word. When she returned the following week, she was able to tell my student that the student had implied the client had consented to sexual relations with her father. The student was mortified. She apologized and told the client she was embarrassed she had said something so insensitive. The client accepted the student's apology, and this incident strengthened the bond between them, which led to further progress for the client.

LISA: *MAKING NEW MUSIC*

At about the time Lisa began remembering the abuse by her father, she became aware of becoming "someone else" to cope with difficult situations. This "someone else" was a part of her that took over when something bad happened. "Someone else" was bold and independent, while Lisa was timid and dependent on the opinions of others. Lisa gave this part of herself the name "The Voice" because she experienced it as an angry, cynical voice in her head.

As we explored the situations in which The Voice was present, we learned that this part of Lisa dated from a time when she would have done anything to please her father. The Voice was the part of Lisa that saw her father's abuse for what it was. Whenever he tried to persuade Lisa to engage in sexual acts with him, The Voice would tell Lisa that her father was evil and that if she went along with him, she would be evil too. The Voice often frightened Lisa enough that she didn't comply with her father's wishes.

Once The Voice was discriminated, so was the timid little girl, who Lisa identified by her childhood nickname, Leesie. Lisa associated this part of herself with feelings of sadness and vulnerability. The little girl's voice was like that of a loon—lonely and sad—and she was able to express this part of herself in her music, which gave it a haunting quality. These two selves were captured in a memory she had of needing to pee. Leesie wanted to pee because she was afraid of being punished for wetting her pants, but The Voice wouldn't let her because she wanted to show her parents that "it's my body, and I'll do what I want with it."

Although The Voice served the very important purpose of protecting Lisa from further abuse, the separation of herself into these parts prevented Lisa from making changes during therapy. The work we did was associated more strongly with one part or the other, and often there would be little transfer of what had been discussed. Leesie had difficulty discussing the abuse by her father and tended to leave those conversations to The Voice. The Voice already had a clear picture; it was Leesie who needed to understand what had happened to her and the impact this continued to have on her life.

The Voice also dominated Lisa's emotional reactions, sometimes to Lisa's detriment. For instance, The Voice was extremely suspicious. She called David "slime" and mocked his efforts to change, which stopped Lisa from learning to trust him. The Voice was also suspicious of me. She told Lisa that therapy was "just a job" for me and that I didn't really care about her. She accused me of repeating Lisa's stories at parties to make myself sound interesting.

Eventually, I learned that The Voice was angry with me for trying to make her disappear. She feared Lisa would no longer need her. I understood this fear as reflecting Lisa's fear of change. I used the metaphor of a piece of music to allay The Voice's fears and to help Lisa integrate the two parts. I talked about The Voice representing one instrument and Leesie representing another. Each instrument could be used to make music, but the music would be more compelling if the instruments were played together, just as her music was enhanced by her friend's instrument. The Voice would never disappear, I explained; she would always be present when Lisa became angry or thought someone was taking advantage of her. Leesie wouldn't disappear either. She would always be present when Lisa felt lonely or vulnerable. Together they would be Lisa, a woman who was sometimes angry and sometimes sad, sometimes strong and sometimes weak.

Lisa's music began to change. At first, she regretted the loss of the haunting music that had been a big part of her identity as a musician. But she soon appreciated the new music she made for its variety and range of expression. What the parts could do together was much greater than what they had been able to do separately. But if she listened carefully, she could still hear the distinct tones of both Leesie and The Voice.

Questions to Ask Yourself
If You Think You Were Abused as a Child

1. What do you remember? Have you ever told anyone? Have you considered the possibility that this is why you experience depression?

2. Do you ever have strong feelings that you've forgotten something important about your childhood? What do you think you might have forgotten? Have you talked about these feelings to anyone?

3. What do you do when you're reminded of the abuse you experienced as a child? Do you drink, take drugs, eat excessive amounts of food, or look for sex? Do you do other things to take your mind off the memories? What would happen if you told someone about the abuse?

4. Are relationships of all kinds so painful for you that you've given up on them? Is it hard to trust relatives, lovers, and friends? Do you feel yourself holding back in these relationships so you don't get hurt?

5. Have you ever felt emotionally abused in a romantic relationship? Has a lover or spouse hit you, pushed you around, or otherwise intimidated you physically? How did you react when these things happened?

6. Sometimes do you feel shame at the very core of your being? Do you feel that you're a bad person at heart and that nothing can change this? Do you expect people to reject you when they figure out how bad you are?

7. If you've sought therapy in the past, how did it go? Did you have difficulty trusting the therapist? Did something happen between you that made you quit therapy?

CHAPTER 8

when the solution is part of the problem

Depressed woman are almost always unhappy with their intimate relationships. For some women, relationship problems seem to have contributed to their depression. For others, depression has taken a toll on their relationship. Women who are both unhappy in their intimate relationships and insecurely attached to their partners are at risk for depression. In this chapter, I describe two patterns in depressed women's intimate relationships. In some couples, both partners have turned down the volume when it comes to their emotional needs. In other couples, one person has turned down the volume while the other has turned it up. These different patterns have different consequences for depressed women.

Relationship problems damage women's self-esteem. They also stop women from getting the support they need when they're stressed. Unhappy couples have great difficulty providing emotional support to one another. For women in these couples, the solution to depression—a close relationship that helps women cope with stress—is part of the problem.

Although most of the research I refer to in this chapter was conducted with married couples, there is every reason to believe that unmarried couples in long-term relationships have similar experiences. Generally, research shows very few differences between married couples and those who live together. At some points in this chapter, I use the labels "husband" and "wife" to distinguish the individual partners. I do so only to simplify my language, and what I say also applies to unmarried couples.

While some of the information in this chapter may be relevant to women's same-sex relationships, there are important differences between heterosexual and homosexual couples. A separate discussion of women's same-sex relationships is beyond the scope of this book. A woman in such a relationship is cautioned that some of the information in this chapter may not be relevant to her situation.

RELATIONSHIP PROBLEMS AND DEPRESSION

Depressed women have a lot of conflict with their intimate partners. Often both partners are easily angered, and they have difficulty talking to each other in a warm, supportive manner, especially when they try to solve problems in their relationship. Not surprisingly, relationship problems increase a woman's risk for depression. Over a one-year period, women who are unhappy in their relationship are three times more likely to develop clinical depression than are women in happy relationships (Whisman and Bruce 1999).

Relationship problems and depression are linked for men too. However, the link is somewhat stronger for women. Women show biological changes, like increased heart rate and increased levels of stress hormones, which show they are more stressed than men are by relationship conflicts. Women also take longer to recover from relationship conflict (Malarkey et al. 1994).

When a woman's depression is treated but her relationship problems are not, she is likely to get depressed again within a short period of time. One of the best predictors of relapse for a woman who has just recovered from depression is her feeling that her partner is critical of her (Hooley and Teasdale 1989). Even if he is not actively critical but behaves in a way that seems to show he does not care about her, she may become increasingly depressed over the following months (Whiffen, Kallos-Lilly, and MacDonald 2001). Conversely, having a warm, supportive partner helps a depressed woman recover quickly (McLeod, Kessler, and Landis 1992). Unfortunately, we will see that for many depressed women, a supportive partner is not available.

CHICKEN OR EGG?

It is rare for me to meet a depressed woman who is happy in her intimate relationship. Although I did not choose them for this reason, all three of the women I included in this book were unhappy in their relationships. However, this does not mean that relationship problems cause depression. Which comes first: depression or relationship problems? In some cases, the woman's depression was a direct result of her relationship problems. As we will see later in this chapter, this was clear in Anne's case. At other times, the relationship problems began after the woman became depressed. Tracy and Matt, for example, got along well and rarely argued before Tracy became depressed.

For most of this chapter, I will talk about the ways in which problems in an intimate relationship can lead to depression. Most of the research has assumed that relationship problems cause depression. However, it is important for women to know that depression almost always has a negative impact on intimate relationships. Relationship problems and depression form a vicious cycle that makes either problem difficult to deal with without addressing the other.

When we are depressed, we see ourselves and the world around us in a negative light. We are sensitive to rejection and criticism. As a result, we often interpret ambiguous interpersonal events in a negative way that makes us feel rejected. One depressed woman's husband would come home from work and immediately check his e-mail. She concluded he was avoiding her. While she may have been correct, it is also possible that he was just checking his e-mail. Depressed women are inclined to assume the worst about their partner's behavior.

Many depressed women are unaware of the impact their depression has on the people who live with them. When we are depressed, we can be very hard to get along with. We can be irritable. Our moods can change abruptly without any apparent cause. We're easily stressed and have difficulty recovering. People who are not depressed can get tired of a depressed person's negativity and pessimism.

Depression tends to be contagious (Joiner and Katz 1999). When we live with a person who is depressed, our own mood becomes more negative over time. Ironically, the closer the couple is, the more likely they are to "catch" one another's depressed mood. An intimate partner may resent his depressed spouse for "bringing him down." Once both partners feel depressed, they are likely to have more conflicts.

The nondepressed partner can have mixed or negative feelings about the depressed woman that he feels he cannot express. For instance, he may feel she is a burden. One depressed woman went to bed whenever she didn't feel well, leaving her husband to make dinner and take care of their children after a day at work. Not surprisingly, he was resentful. The nondepressed partner may be caught between feeling sympathy for the depressed woman's emotional distress and annoyance with her depressed behavior. Often the nondepressed partner's anger leaks out in a sharp tone of voice or a resigned sigh. A depressed woman picks up on these subtle cues and concludes that her partner is fed up with her.

Depressed women also have negative expectations of their partners. For instance, they expect them to be unsupportive and critical. This expectation leads depressed women to behave negatively toward their partners. Over time their own negative behavior adds both to their relationship problems and to their feelings of depression (Davila et al. 1997).

Tracy: *"You* Never *Support Me"*

Tracy had an ongoing conflict with Matt's parents about their unfenced pool. Quite rightly, she was concerned Michael could fall into the pool. However, she handled this situation by demanding that Matt's father put in a fence if he wanted to see his grandson. She gave him this ultimatum after a Sunday dinner at Matt's parents' house but without consulting Matt or getting his opinion about how best to handle his father. Matt was caught off guard and said nothing while they were at his parents' house. Afterward he told Tracy he agreed with her concern but disagreed with the way she had talked to his father. They had a fight. When I asked Tracy why she did not discuss her concerns with Matt beforehand, she told me that Matt "never" supported her. She explained that he always took his father's side against her and that she knew she would have to deal with the problem on her own. Tracy assumed Matt would be unsupportive, so she broadsided his father, which led to a fight that confirmed her assumption that Matt would be unsupportive.

TURNING THE VOLUME UP OR DOWN IN ROMANTIC RELATIONSHIPS

As discussed in chapter 5, John Bowlby (1969, 1973, 1980) believed that the need to feel connected to and accepted by the people who are important to us is a basic human need that is present throughout our lives. Although he based attachment theory on his observations of babies and children, he maintained that humans of all ages need to feel securely attached.

Research psychologists Cindy Hazan and Phil Shaver (1987) wondered if in Western societies, romantic partners function as *attachment figures* for each other. An attachment figure is someone to whom a person turns for help, advice, and emotional support as well as comfort when they are hurt, ill, or distressed. Hazan and Shaver did a study to see if the attachment strategies that children use with their caregivers also can be seen in adult romantic relationships. They were right. Adults in intimate relationships show the same patterns of secure and insecure attachment that babies and children do with their parents. Sue Johnson and I reviewed the resulting research literature to create thumbnail sketches of securely and insecurely attached adults [in romantic relationships] (Johnson and Whiffen 1999). I describe what we found in the following sections.

Adults who are *securely* attached to their romantic partners believe they are lovable and that their romantic partners will respond to them when needed. They trust their partners and enjoy being close to them. Securely attached people are usually aware of what they are feeling, and they communicate their feelings and needs clearly to their partners. They are able to ask for comfort and support. Even when they are angry with their partners, they express their feelings constructively and in a way that does not damage the relationship. Generally, securely attached people are happy with their relationships and not at risk for depression. Although they can experience relationship problems, usually they are able to solve these problems without getting outside help.

Turning Up the Volume

As is the case with babies and children, some *insecurely* attached adults turn up the volume in their intimate relationships. These people are worried about being rejected or abandoned by romantic partners. Anxiety makes them sensitive to any sign of rejection, which means they are often jealous and easily angered by their partner's behavior. When they are angry, they tend to demand reassurance or to blame and criticize romantic partners. They experience intense, overwhelming emotions that they express with force. Because they have difficulty focusing on anything but their own emotions, they can have trouble seeing events from their partner's point of view.

One depressed woman was hurt that her husband played golf on the weekend and left her alone with their young children. She felt he devalued her work as a mother and dismissed her need to relax away from their children. Instead of expressing her hurt, however, she would call him a "jerk" and accuse him of being bored with her. Needless to say, this strategy created conflict in their relationship.

People who turn up the volume in their intimate relationships may have experienced rejection as children, or they may feel rejected and criticized by their current romantic partner. Sometimes they experienced rejection in both relationships. For instance, the golf-playing husband told his wife that he deserved to have his leisure time because he worked hard all week, while she spent her time shopping and having lunch with her friends. She was justified in feeling that he was critical and demeaning of her.

Turning Down the Volume

Some insecurely attached adults turn down the volume in their intimate relationships. They have taken their anxiety about romantic partners one step further than the person who turns up the volume: They think it is just a matter of time before their partner rejects or abandons them, and they behave in ways that will protect them from feeling hurt when this happens. They minimize their expectations of their partner and keep as much emotional distance as possible. They are uncomfortable with intimacy and prefer not to tell their partner much. They also are uncomfortable when their partner tries to be intimate.

A person who has turned down the volume is most likely to withdraw from their partner when they feel stressed or upset. They do not want to show their partner that they are in need because they have learned in this or other relationships that neediness is a sign of weakness. They do not want to talk about their feelings, and they do not want to be held or comforted. One depressed woman refused to let her husband help with any housework or child care, despite being overwhelmed by her job and caring for their children. At her insistence, he was already living in their basement, and she believed he would eventually leave her. She told me that if she let him help her now, she would not be able to cope once he was gone.

People who have turned down the volume do not like to talk about their relationship problems. Often they deny there is a problem or that they are unhappy. Whenever their partner tries to bring up problems, they do whatever they can to avoid the discussion. One husband had the ability to fall asleep in the middle of these discussions with his wife. People who have turned down the volume can still get angry with their partners, but often they are unaware of their anger. They express anger indirectly, for instance, by getting a headache and going to bed. Someone who has muted their own feelings also has difficulty recognizing emotions in other people, with the result that they can be unempathic.

Women who turn down the volume in intimate relationships may have had indifferent parents or they may be involved with an emotionally cold romantic partner at present. The depressed woman who wouldn't let her husband help out was married to a man who was, at times, breathtakingly insensitive to her. Once she was injured while they were hiking. He got her medical attention then left her alone in a hotel for five days while he finished the hike because he had been "looking forward to it all summer."

Disorganization in Intimate Relationships

Some people are inconsistent in their intimate relationships. They may alternate between feeling enraged with their romantic partners for not being emotionally responsive and feeling distant and disengaged. In both states, their feelings toward their partners are intense. The way they flip from one extreme to the other is confusing for partners. Their intimate relationships are tumultuous.

With one depressed woman, I had to check at the beginning of each session to see if she was still dating her boyfriend; they could break up three times in a single week. Their breakups were brought on by minor disagreements that would not cause conflict in most relationships. For instance, one breakup happened because her boyfriend disagreed with her opinion of a movie. She felt the argument reflected fundamental and irreconcilable differences between them, and she could not bear to be with someone who was so different from her. At other times, she was repulsed by the idea of physical intimacy with him. Depressed women who are disorganized in their intimate relationships usually experienced sexual or physical abuse when they were children (Cassidy and Mohr 2001).

COUPLE PATTERNS WHEN WOMEN ARE DEPRESSED

When a woman is depressed and her relationship is troubled, I typically see one of two patterns.

Both Partners Turn Down the Volume

Mostly commonly, both partners have turned down the volume in their relationship. The depressed woman believes that rejection or abandonment by her partner is inevitable. She keeps an emotional distance from him to protect herself from getting hurt. When she does feel hurt by him, she is more likely to stop talking to him than she is to tell him how she feels or to start a fight with him.

Her husband also has turned down the volume, possibly in response to her depression and their conflict, or possibly because this is his preference in intimate relationships. Women who are prone to depression are often involved with men who are cold, unemotional, reserved, and lacking in compassion (Daley and Hammen 2002). Needless to say, these men are not very responsive to depressed women's emotional needs. Being married to a man who has turned down the volume makes women's depression worse over time (Whiffen, Kallos-Lilly, and MacDonald 2001).

When the woman expresses vulnerable feelings or looks for comfort and reassurance from her husband, he is uncomfortable. Sometimes he rejects the woman outright by telling her not to be "silly." Sometimes he changes the topic or does not respond to what she has said. His lack of responsiveness feeds the depressed woman's fear that he will eventually reject or abandon her (Whiffen 2005). In this way, the husband's behavior contributes to his wife's depression. This is an especially toxic cycle. This woman may stay depressed until her husband becomes more responsive to her or their relationship ends.

From working with these couples and doing research, I have learned that the husband's lack of responsiveness does not mean he does not care about his wife (Whiffen 2005). Typically, these men are uncomfortable with intimacy. They feel uncomfortable expressing their feelings, especially feelings like love, tenderness, sadness, or weakness. When their wives turn to them for comfort and reassurance, these men don't know what to do. They are embarrassed. For instance, the husband who continued the hiking trip without her said that expressing tender feelings for his wife made him feel weak. Staying with her at the hotel would have been "mushy," like something a Harlequin romance hero would do.

When I work with couples in therapy, I use emotionally focused couple therapy, which I'll discuss further in chapter 10. This therapy aims to improve the couple's attachment bond. I encourage husbands to talk to their wives about their attachment needs. Usually, these husbands care deeply for their wives and they want to be close to them, but they have difficulty talking about their feelings or showing them. Ideally, I hope to make the husband feel comfortable with both his own and his wife's attachment needs, including their needs to be comforted and reassured when they feel vulnerable.

Very occasionally, it becomes apparent to me that the unresponsive husband really doesn't care about his depressed wife. This is not common when the couple comes for therapy. Most husbands who are willing to come for couple therapy love their wives and want the relationship to succeed. Even when I work with women individually, I do not usually sense that their husbands are genuinely uncaring. Usually, a man who is willing to stay with his depressed wife cares deeply about her. However, on occasion I have seen husbands who do not seem to love their depressed wives. These women have to consider the possibility that they may need to leave the relationship to stop feeling depressed.

One Partner Turns the Volume Up, and the Other Turns It Down

This pattern, which is common among unhappy couples, is called the *pursue-withdraw* pattern because one person does the chasing while the other runs away. From the point of view of attachment theory, both partners are concerned about being rejected or abandoned by their spouse, but one copes by turning up the volume while the other copes by turning it down. One partner is angry, blaming, and critical; the other is cold and unresponsive.

The depressed woman could be either partner. As I describe later in this chapter, Lisa was the withdrawn partner in her relationship with David, while Anne was the pursuing partner in her relationship with Bill. However, the consequences for depressed women are very different in the two situations.

David's pursuit of Lisa was reassuring to her. She never doubted that he cared for her. Because she believed in his love, she was able to use her relationship with him to stop feeling depressed. Once he accepted her abuse history, he was able to be a more supportive and caring husband. Generally, relationship problems are easier to resolve if the depressed wife has turned down the volume and the husband has turned it up. Changing the way they interact with each other has a dramatic impact on the wife's depression. The goal here is to draw the depressed woman out so that she expresses her attachment needs, and her partner has the chance to respond supportively.

In contrast, Bill's withdrawal from Anne fed her fears that she was not good enough, which contributed to her depression. These couples face greater challenges. A depressed wife who has turned up the volume when it comes to her attachment needs can be harsh, critical, and angry with her husband, which makes it harder to get him to risk telling her about his feelings. When he does take a chance, she may attack him.

The golf-playing husband, for instance, turned out to be intimidated by his wife. Although what he said seemed to devalue her contribution to their family, in fact he felt insecure about his own contribution. It was very important to him that he provide a good income for her and their children, but his business was in danger of failing. He was afraid to tell her about his business worries because he thought she would think less of him. When he played golf every weekend, he was escaping. He was avoiding his worries about the business and avoiding conversation with his wife, who he feared would learn the truth about the business if she was around him long enough to question him closely. This husband's fear that his wife would think less of him had a basis in reality. The first time he talked about his fears in a couple therapy session, his wife told him that his business was failing because he was a "wimp" who let people take advantage of him.

Although both partners in pursue-withdraw couples tend to be depressed (Whiffen, Kallos-Lilly, and MacDonald 2001), often the man's depression is not obvious when they start therapy. As I draw the husband out and get him to talk to me and his partner about his attachment needs, he begins to express feelings of inadequacy, particularly in his intimate relationship.

Again, my goal with these couples is to help the husband to express his attachment needs. Often men who have turned down the volume are afraid they will be criticized by their wives if they tell them how they really feel. In fact, their wives usually are sympathetic to their husband's feelings of insecurity or inadequacy. The wife's anger and criticism reflect her anxiety about being rejected or abandoned by him. Once she realizes that he cares deeply about her and is not going to reject her, she is less angry and more supportive. He, in turn, becomes more communicative.

ECHOES FROM THE PAST

As I discussed in chapter 7, childhood sexual abuse has a special impact on intimate relationships. Many women with this history avoid having intimate relationships at all. One depressed client was an attractive woman in her midforties. As an adult, she had had only one "romantic" relationship, with a man she met once or twice a month for sex. Women with an abuse history are more likely than other women to divorce or never marry.

If they do establish an intimate relationship, they are likely to have problems with intimacy and sexuality. They say they always need to be in control and that they can never let down their guard with their partner. As we saw with Lisa, the inability to trust is a major problem. We cannot be truly intimate with another person if we cannot trust them to be gentle with our soft spots. Not surprisingly, women who were sexually abused as children have great difficulty forming secure attachment relationships. Women who were abused by a family member are likely to be disorganized in attachment relationships (Alexander 1993).

These women also experience many sexual problems. Often they are dissatisfied with their sexual relations. They feel a lot of shame, fear, anxiety, and guilt about sex. In addition, they may have difficulty becoming aroused or they may experience pain with intercourse. Sexual activity can lead to flashbacks about the abuse. Sexual problems are especially likely when a woman was abused by someone in her family.

Lisa experienced many difficulties in her sexual relationship with David. She felt sadistically abused by him during lovemaking. I was never able to get a clear picture of what he did that made her feel this way because she never wanted to discuss specifics. It's possible she interpreted ambiguous sexual events as abusive. It also is possible that from the beginning of their relationship she tolerated rougher sex with David than she liked because she was used to having sex that hurt.

Clinicians say that the romantic partners of women with a sexual abuse history feel frustrated, rejected, lonely, and inadequate. They may be exhausted by what they see as the sexually abused partner's unending demands for support. If the woman is disorganized in her intimate relationships, partners can feel like a yo-yo: first pursued then pushed away.

Intimate relationships are even more important to a woman who was sexually abused as a child than they are to other women. These women are both better protected by a good relationship and more vulnerable to depression when their relationship is not good (Whiffen, Judd, and Aube 1999). Yet it is difficult for these women to see their relationships except through the lens of their abuse. Dissatisfaction with the current relationship can be part of the reason that women with a sexual abuse history become depressed. However, dealing only with the current relationship is unlikely to provide anything more than temporary relief. Lisa first came to therapy because of relationship problems. If I had tried to work only with her immediate relationship problems, I might have helped her recover from that particular episode of depression but she soon would have become depressed again.

Lisa and David: *A Pursue-Withdraw Couple*

As Lisa had done with her parents, she turned down the volume in her relationship with David. She had no expectation that he would be responsive to her emotional needs, and, as a result, she made no demands on him. She was distant and mistrusting. David had turned the volume up. He was argumentative and critical of her.

When they were first seen by their couple therapist, Lisa was unable to see David as anyone but another abusive man. However, the therapist was able to get Lisa to express her anger toward David, and David, to his credit, was able to take responsibility for things he had done to hurt Lisa. Once he became a more supportive partner, Lisa quickly finished her individual therapy.

I never met David. However, from what Lisa told me about their couple therapy, I wondered if he felt as many husbands of sexually abused women do: frustrated, rejected, and lonely. I do not know why he had affairs. But unlike many men who have affairs, David did nothing to hide what he was doing. I wondered if David wanted Lisa to know about his affairs because he wanted to get a reaction from her. I wondered if this was his way of turning up the volume. Although this does not excuse David for having affairs, it does help us understand why he had them.

WHY RELATIONSHIP PROBLEMS LEAD TO DEPRESSION

Relationship problems have an impact on women's self-esteem and on their ability to seek and receive the support they need when they are stressed. Both factors put women at risk for depression.

What's Wrong with Me?

Relationship problems are bad for women's self-esteem (Culp and Beach 1998). Women who are unhappy in their relationships feel inadequate. They feel they have failed at an important life task. Their low self-esteem puts them at risk for depression. But why do relationship problems make women feel bad about themselves? Why don't they blame the problem on their husbands? Why don't they shrug their shoulders and put the failing relationship down to a bad choice?

According to Dana Jack's (1991) silencing the self theory, which I discussed in chapter 4, many women's self-esteem is dependent on their ability to create and maintain good intimate relationships. They may *self-silence* to create the illusion that the relationship is happier than it actually is. Self-silencing involves suppressing feelings of anger and thoughts that might threaten the relationship, such as thoughts that their partner is wrong, selfish, or unreasonable. This strategy may be adaptive in the short term because it reduces conflict. A husband cannot argue with a wife who agrees with everything he says. However, in the long run, self-silencing may put women at risk for depression.

In my clinical experience, self-silencing creates a blind spot about relationship problems. When we do not talk about a feeling or problem, it does not seem quite real to us. A part of the woman may know she is unhappy in her relationship, but another part is busy denying the problem and reinterpreting feelings of unhappiness. For these women, admitting unhappiness is equivalent to admitting failure as a woman. Like Lisa and Anne, they find themselves in intolerable relationships they can neither change nor leave.

Women are especially likely to silence themselves when their husbands are critical of them (Thompson, Whiffen, and Aube 2001). A woman who is constantly criticized inevitably becomes critical of herself (Whiffen and Aube 1999). Like the child who is always told she is doing something wrong, the criticized wife anticipates her husband's criticism and tries to avoid it by being self-critical.

I think that men are more critical of their partners when they are insecurely attached in the relationship. Men's criticism of their female partners can be their way of turning up the volume.

One depressed woman tried to be as mild as possible to avoid her husband's criticism. But no matter how quiet, timid, and submissive she was around him, he always found something to criticize. Most of the time, his criticism was trivial. She bought the wrong brand of toothpaste, or she left hamburgers cooling on the counter while she made a salad. She would never argue with him, but over the years she became convinced she was deeply flawed. After seeing me in individual therapy for a few months, she decided she wanted to leave him, but she was too afraid to tell him. I agreed to a session in which she would tell him how she felt. To this woman's surprise, her husband was delighted to be included in one of our sessions. His eyes filled with tears as he told me how afraid he was that she didn't love him and would eventually leave him. Suddenly I realized that his constant criticism of her was his very destructive way of turning up the volume. Sadly, realization came too late for this couple, and she left him anyway.

Anne: *From Self-Silencing to Self-Criticism*

Anne grew up being criticized by her mother. Later she married Bill, an emotionally distant man who criticized her flamboyance and zest for life. She accepted his criticism because he echoed her self-criticism. As I described in chapter 4, she changed everything she could about herself to please him.

Because Bill was in the military, they moved a lot. Anne would feel sad and lonely after these moves. She would feel tired of always starting over. However, like many husbands of depressed women, Bill was not very supportive of her. He had turned down the volume. He was uncomfortable with intimacy and unresponsive to Anne's attachment needs. When she expressed her feelings to Bill, he would tell her she was "weak" and "dependent." He would tell her to "buck up" and get on with her life. People who have turned down the volume feel uncomfortable with weakness and vulnerability, even when it is expressed by someone else.

In both her first family and her marriage, Anne had learned that she sometimes could get the response she craved by turning up the volume. She learned that if she "fell apart," Bill would take her feelings seriously and, for a brief time, become more attentive. When she fell apart, Anne finally felt connected to her husband. However, connection came at a steep price: becoming weak, dependent, and needy.

By the time I met Anne, she believed what Bill had told her about herself. In the beginning, she often told me she was "needy." I had a hard time matching this word to the stern woman who sat with a ramrod-straight back in front of me. She didn't look needy. She looked cold and hard. She would explain to me that Bill's ability to pick up and leave people and places was "mature," while her sense of loss reflected her childishness. Anne had accepted Bill's criticism of her and made it her own, even though it was utterly inconsistent with the person she had become.

Anne's self-esteem was entirely dependent on getting Bill's approval. She had made many compromises in their relationship, and a part of the real Anne had been washed away with each one. Anne no longer knew who she was, what she wanted in life, even what she liked and disliked. When she lost the relationship, Anne lost her identity.

A BARREN MARRIAGE

I expected Anne to come out of her depression as she realized that although the marriage was over, she now had the freedom to be herself. As the months wore on and her depression did not improve, I began to worry. Anne knew she had to move on. She would tell me that if she could only file for divorce and return to her hometown, she would feel better. But she couldn't. Why was she stuck? I knew she was not stuck because she loved Bill. She never longed for him. Their meetings were brief and businesslike. I began to suspect there was something in a blind spot she was not telling me.

One day I asked Anne to imagine Bill sitting in an empty chair in my office. I asked her to tell the empty chair how she felt. I don't use this exercise very often because I find my clients are uncomfortable with it. They can't really let their imaginations go. I had forgotten that Anne was an actress.

Anne began to talk to the empty chair. This was an Anne I had never seen before. She wept. Her voice shook and she trembled. She sounded like a little girl pleading with a parent to love her. Then she became angry. Her fists clenched and her jaw tightened. She told Bill their relationship had been empty and now the emptiness was inside her. She told him he had stolen her life. He had stolen the meaning from her existence and given nothing in return. He had taken it away by stopping her from becoming a wife and mother. I wasn't sure what she meant, so I asked her to tell Bill how he had done that, and she began to sob. She cried and pounded the empty chair with her fists. She pounded so hard that two decades of institutional dust exploded out of the upholstery and swirled in the air. She was choking on the dust and wailing and shouting at him, and all of a sudden, I understood. Their relationship had never been consummated.

This was Anne's blind spot.

Anne started to laugh. She was laughing because the chair in my office was so dirty and because she was making so much noise. She joked that the other people in my hallway would expect an Amazon to leave my office. She laughed and laughed and then she cried, softly this time. She cried as she told me she was a virgin when she married Bill. She had had sexual feelings for him, but she had been so naïve that she had no idea how to act on them. Bill had tried to make love to her a few times during their honeymoon, but each time was unsuccessful. He had never tried again. Anne didn't know how to talk about the problem. She didn't know what to talk about. After ten years of marriage, she screwed up her courage to ask Bill why he didn't make love to her. He told her he didn't find her attractive, and she never asked again.

Anne had never told anyone her secret. She was too ashamed. She accepted Bill's explanation that the problem was her fault. To say she was moved by my sympathy is an understatement. She was astounded that anyone could see it from her point of view. Her self-criticism was so absolute that she didn't even have sympathy for herself.

After this session, Anne went through a period of real mourning. She did not mourn the loss of her relationship with Bill as much as the loss of the life it was now too late to have. Anne would never be a mother, but it wasn't too late for her to experience a sexually intimate relationship. A few months later, she began dating a man. As their relationship moved toward sexual intimacy, she was afraid and ashamed. She worried what this man would think of a virgin divorcée. When she finally got up the nerve to tell him, he was deeply sympathetic. Not long after that, Anne told me she no longer needed to come to our sessions.

I never met Bill, and I have no idea what his story is. Maybe he is gay. Maybe Anne was the wrong woman for him. The important thing was for Anne to understand that Bill's rejection of her had nothing to do with her. Like unhappily married parents who yell at their kids, Bill had his own problems. His criticism of Anne reflected his own deep unhappiness, not Anne's unworthiness.

When the Solution Is Part of the Problem

As I discussed in chapter 3, intimate relationships are protective for women. Women who have at least one person in whom they can confide are at much lower risk for depression than are women who lack a *confidante* (Brown and Harris 1978). A confidante can be anyone: a friend, a relative, a parent, an adult child, a lover, or a spouse. What is important is that this person provides comfort, reassurance, and support, especially during stressful times. In our society, a woman's primary confidante is likely to be her romantic partner or spouse. Increasingly the ideal romantic relationship has included friendship.

On average, men are not as good as women are at providing emotional support. Men focus on solving problems, and they can be frustrated with women's need to discuss a situation in detail without coming to a solution. Both sexes prefer to talk to a woman when they are stressed or troubled. So the average woman is operating with an emotional support deficit: she gives more emotional support to her romantic partner than she receives from him. A man who is the sole source of emotional support for a woman may not be enough. To compensate, she needs to turn to other confidantes. In a mobile society, friends and family may not be available.

From the beginning, romantic relationships pose a risk to girls' well-being. The mere act of becoming involved in a romantic relationship increases an adolescent girl's risk for depression, in part because having a boyfriend has a negative impact on the girl's relationship with her parents (Joyner and Udry 2000). A girl who transfers her needs for emotional support from her parents to her boyfriend may find he lacks the maturity or the skill to be her confidante.

When couples have problems, husbands are even less likely than usual to provide support to their wives. Relationship problems decrease the amount of support couples give each other. Unhappy men, in particular, often withdraw emotionally from their partners. When women are in a relationship with an emotionally distant man, they begin to feel needy and dependent, which increases their risk for depression (Whiffen and Aube 1999). For these women, the solution to their depression—an intimate relationship that helps them deal with stress— is part of the problem.

For many years, researchers believed that any woman in a troubled intimate relationship was at risk for depression. However, recent research has shown that they are at risk only if they also are insecurely attached (Scott and Cordova 2002). Not all people who are unhappy in their relationships are insecurely attached to each other; you can be unhappy with your partner's behavior but still believe that he loves and cares for you. Interestingly, attachment insecurity is only a risk factor for depression when the woman is stressed (Hammen et al. 1995). Insecurely attached women, especially those who have turned down the volume when it comes to their emotional needs, may lack the close relationships that protect them from becoming depressed when they experience life stress.

Tracy and Matt: *Separate Checks*

Tracy grew up in a family where her emotional needs were neglected. She learned to solve her own problems and to take care of other people as a way of being connected to them. For an intimate partner she chose Matt, a man who was used to being physically cared for but who otherwise made few demands on her. Before their son Michael was born, the relationship worked for both of them. Tracy took care of making money and paying their bills; Matt was a friend and companion. Although they were in an intimate relationship, both were more involved with their first families than they were with each other. Both had turned down the volume in their relationship.

Then Tracy hit the wall that is motherhood. Like many new mothers, she was overwhelmed—by the physical labor involved in caring for an infant and by the responsibility. Most new mothers turn to their romantic partners for support. They expect their partners to take over housework, cooking, and the care of older children. They look to their partners for emotional support. Especially if they are new to motherhood or if the baby is more difficult than expected, they look to their partners for feedback that they are doing a good job (Whiffen 2004).

Instead of looking to Matt, Tracy looked to her family. Unfortunately, her mother and sister couldn't meet her needs. In therapy sessions, I began to wonder out loud why Tracy never turned to Matt. Tracy told me she was confused about Matt's feelings for her. On the one hand, he told her he loved her. In the mornings when he went to work, he would cut flowers and put them in a vase on the table for her. However, he never put his dirty breakfast dishes into the dishwasher. He never cleaned up after himself or did any housework or cooking. Before the baby was born, this division of labor had not bothered Tracy, but now she had too many other things to cope with. Before the baby was born, they were "separate checks." Now Tracy wanted Matt to be part of a team with her.

MATT FEELS IRRELEVANT

At this point, I suggested Tracy and Matt might find couple therapy helpful. Tracy agreed, and to her surprise, so did Matt. I didn't see them as a couple because I already had a relationship with Tracy. I was concerned Matt would feel that I sympathized more with her point of view than with his. However, I agreed to supervise their couple therapy, which was done with a young man named Rick who was learning couple therapy under my supervision.

As the father of a young child, Rick was sensitive to what the issues might be for Matt. With Rick's help, Matt was able to tell Tracy how irrelevant he felt. Tracy was a great mother. Michael was strongly attached to her and would cry whenever he was left alone with his dad. Matt didn't know how to be a father to Michael, but there was an even more important reason that he felt irrelevant. He had brought up getting married now that they had a child together, but Tracy had told him they didn't need "a piece of paper" to be a family. Matt was afraid she didn't want to marry him. He worried that all she wanted from him was a baby. Now that she had Michael, she didn't need him anymore. Working long hours seemed to be the only contribution he could make.

Tracy was very moved by what Matt said. She knew Matt felt excluded, but instead of empathizing with his feelings, she had criticized him for not spending enough time with his son. She confessed she had worried he worked long hours to avoid his family in the same way that her mother had done. Hearing that he felt shut out and irrelevant made her realize how much he did care. Tracy told Matt she wanted to be able to share her load with him, but she felt she could not trust him to help her when she needed him.

TRACY'S ATTACHMENT INJURY

Tracy admitted she had never believed she could count on Matt. She didn't believe any woman could count on a man. In Tracy's experience, men were unreliable. She had given Matt one chance to be there when she needed him, and he had let her down.

It had happened in the hospital after she delivered Michael. There were complications after her delivery, and she was moved from the maternity ward to the intensive care unit. Tracy was panic-stricken. Convinced she was going to die, she asked Matt to spend the night by her side. Matt told her she wouldn't die as long as she was in the hospital. He told her he was exhausted after being awake for two days during Michael's delivery. He told her he needed to go home and sleep.

This incident is an example of what is called an *attachment injury*. An attachment injury happens in an intimate relationship when a person is desperate for her partner to comfort and reassure her (Johnson, Makinen, and Millikin 2001). Often the desperate partner feels the situation is a matter of life and death, as Tracy did. She may feel that her very survival depends on her partner's response. But the partner does not respond in the way she needs. He may be caught up in the situation too. Or he may not realize how important the moment is to her. Because the moment is so emotionally loaded for the desperate partner, it immediately changes her view of the relationship in a way that is difficult to reverse.

When Matt left Tracy alone at the hospital, she was devastated. She had never asked for his help before. Because he was not available at such an important moment in her life, she believed he would never be available. She was so hurt, she didn't give him another chance to let her down.

Matt knew Tracy was upset about his leaving the hospital. They had had many fights about it. Couples often fight over and over again about attachment injuries without being able to resolve them. But until their session with Rick, Matt did not understand what the incident had meant to Tracy.

Matt admitted he had been worried about Tracy at the hospital. He was used to Tracy being strong and in control. When she became "hysterical," he was convinced something really was wrong with her. His own fear was so intense that he was unable to comfort her. He just wanted to run away. He admitted he "screwed up" in leaving the hospital. He told Tracy he realized he had made a mistake as soon as he left, and he had been trying to make it up to her ever since. He told her that, if he could, he would take back what had happened "in a heartbeat."

Both Tracy and Matt had turned down the volume in their relationship because they were uncomfortable with feelings of vulnerability. For Tracy, this discomfort was born of a lifetime of experiences with unreliable people. I am not sure what factors led to this discomfort for Matt. When Michael was born, Tracy's self-reliance raised Matt's fears that he was irrelevant. In fear, he withdrew. Tracy interpreted Matt's unresponsiveness to mean that he didn't care about her, a perception that was confirmed when he didn't change anything about his life to accommodate their new baby. Tracy already feared that her mother and sister did not care about her. Believing that Matt did not care either was a significant factor in her becoming depressed.

THE VICIOUS CYCLE

Depression and relationship distress can form a vicious cycle that is difficult to untangle. If a woman's depression is treated but her relationship problems are not, she will soon become depressed again. If the relationship problems are treated without exploring the impact that her episodes of depression have on the couple, the relationship will falter again. As I will discuss in more detail in chapter 10, I encourage couples whose relationship problems wax and wane with depression to consider couple therapy.

Questions to Ask Yourself

1. Do I avoid romantic relationships? If so, why? What has been my experience in past relationships? (If you're not presently in a romantic relationship, you might want to answer the following questions about your past relationships.)

2. Am I happy in my marriage or romantic relationship? Was I happy before I became depressed? Does my relationship play a part in my depression? How?

3. Do I feel securely attached to my partner or spouse? If I'm insecurely attached, do I generally turn up the volume or turn it down? Do I sometimes do both? What impact does this seem to have on my partner?

4. Does my partner feel securely attached to me? Does my partner turn up the volume or turn it down? Does my partner sometimes do both? How does that make me feel?

5. Which adjective in each of the following pairs describes my partner in relationship to me: supportive or critical, interested or indifferent, warm or cold, sensitive or insensitive, outgoing or reserved, compassionate or judgmental? Is my partner responsive to me when I express feelings of love, tenderness, sadness, or vulnerability?

6. What impact does my depression have on my relationship? Am I sensitive to rejection by my partner? Am I irritable or moody with my partner? Am I easily stressed by things that happen? Do I take out my stress on my partner? Does my mood seem to bring my partner down? Does my partner sometimes seem to have mixed feelings about me? What part do my expectations for my partner play in our conflicts?

7. Do I blame myself for our problems? Do I feel like a failure in relationships?

8. Do I keep my thoughts and feelings to myself to avoid conflict with my partner?

9. Is my partner a confidante? Do I have other confidantes? Who can I talk to when I'm mad at my partner?

10. Has something happened in our relationship that I can't seem to get over? Do I feel really hurt about this event? Does it keep coming up whenever we fight?

CHAPTER 9

like mother, like child

Children whose mothers have a history of depression are different from other kids. They do less well in most ways, and they are different from other children at all ages, from infancy through adulthood. They differ in their emotional well-being, how well they do at school, their friendships with other children, and the ways they interact with their families. Some of these differences may stem from the fact that these children may have the genetic or neurobiological risk for depression. In addition, depressed mothers' relationships with their children may contribute to their children's emotional problems. When we look at the big picture, we can see that the lives of depressed women and their children are stressful in many ways. These contextual factors may contribute more to children's emotional problems than does the mother's depression in and of itself.

Mothers who have experienced depression can help protect their children from depression. Several strategies have been shown to be effective ways of dealing with children's negative feelings. These strategies help children build skills that can stop them from becoming depressed.

CHILDREN OF DEPRESSED MOTHERS ARE DIFFERENT

Sherryl Goodman and Ian Gotlib (1999) reviewed the research on the children of depressed mothers. As babies, many children with depressed mothers are *temperamentally difficult*. That is, they cry a lot and they are hard to soothe. A baby who is difficult may have trouble developing a secure attachment relationship with his or her caregivers. As these children get older, they are easily upset or angered. They seem to be stressed by things that don't bother other children. They also have trouble calming down once they are upset. They may need more help from their parents than other children do to cope with stress and bad feelings.

When the children of depressed mothers go to school, they have more trouble making and keeping friends, so they may not have as many friends as other kids. They may have more fights with the friends they do have, or these friendships may seem more fragile. They also don't do as well at school as other children do. Not surprisingly, they don't feel as good about themselves.

By the time they reach adolescence, the kids of depressed mothers are more likely than other children to have emotional problems. These problems take one of two forms. Kids can be angry and act out by smoking cigarettes, using drugs and alcohol, disobeying rules, getting into fights, and running away. Or they can be depressed and anxious. The children of depressed mothers are at risk for both types of emotional difficulty. Daughters seem to be at particular risk for depression. One study showed that almost half of the daughters of depressed parents experience an episode of depression before the age of nineteen (Wickramarantne and Weissman 1998).

The impact on children is greater when the mother's depression occurs earlier in the children's lives. Children's development is cumulative; what comes earlier provides the basis for what comes later. A mother who experiences postpartum depression may have trouble forming a secure attachment relationship with her baby. Insecure attachment can have an impact on the child's ability to feel comfortable with others and self-confident as she moves into the world. In contrast, if the mother's first episode of depression occurs during her daughter's adolescence, her daughter already will have developed as an individual, so the impact of her mother's depression will be minimized.

Another important factor is how much depression the mother experiences during her kids' childhood and adolescence. The risk to a child is greater if the mother is depressed for longer periods of time and/or more often.

CHICKEN OR EGG?

Which comes first: the mother's depression or the child's problems? Most of the research has assumed that the mother's depression has a negative impact on the child. However, children who are temperamentally difficult—easily irritated and stressed, and hard to calm down—who have problems with friends, or are not doing well at school are likely to contribute to their mothers' feelings of depression.

Being a good mother is an important part of women's gender role. Most of us value being mothers, and we feel stressed and guilty when we think we are failing in this role. Mothers have no way of judging whether they are a success except by the outcome. If our children are developing well as people and seem happy, we must be doing a good job. On the other hand, if our children are struggling, it's easy for us to think we must not be very good mothers. While it's unlikely that such a simple link exists between how we parent and who our children are, most mothers take responsibility for both their children's successes and their failures. A difficult child is bound to have an impact on a woman's self-confidence as a parent.

Most of the research has looked at children and their depressed mothers at one point in time, so we don't know what the child was like before the mother became depressed. The rare research that has followed mothers and their children over time showed that mothers' and children's depressed moods fed into one another (Hammen, Burge, and Adrian 1991). A child who is struggling can contribute to her mother's depression.

THREE SOURCES OF RISK

There are at least three different ways that a mother's depression can pose a risk to her children.

It's in the Genes

Some children inherit the genetic risk for depression. The more depression there is in the extended family, the more likely children are to have inherited the combination of genes that predisposes depression. The genetic risk often shows up initially as anxiety (Kovacs and Devlin 1998). At-risk children may have more fears than other children. Sometimes they are afraid of things that most children don't worry about. For instance, some anxious children say they're afraid whenever they're separated from their parents that something terrible will happen and they will never see them again. Most children don't have this fear. Children who are anxious, who are easily upset or angered, who have difficulty being soothed or calming down once they are upset, or who are fearful and withdrawn in new situations and with people they don't know may have the genetic risk for depression.

However, having the genes is usually not enough to develop depression. As I discussed in chapter 2, life stress needs to happen for depression to occur. Even children with a high genetic risk are unlikely to become depressed before adolescence. During childhood, parents have the opportunity to inoculate their children against depression by helping them manage their negative feelings and use relationships to cope with stress. I discuss what can be done to help children later in this chapter.

Childbearing Depression

Some children develop a risk for depression while they are still in their mother's womb. During pregnancy, a woman's biochemistry is intimately linked to that of her fetus. A woman who is stressed and depressed during pregnancy transfers to her baby a significant amount of the stress hormone, cortisol, that is circulating in her bloodstream. At birth, half of the cortisol in the baby's system can be accounted for by the mother's cortisol levels (Field et al. 2004). As I discussed in chapter 2, chronically high levels of cortisol may lead to depression. In fact, the newborns of depressed women show abnormal brain wave activity that is very similar to that of chronically depressed adults (Field et al. 2002). These babies cry more than others, and they make more angry and sad faces. Depression during pregnancy may permanently change the baby's neurobiology so that these children are more reactive to stress later in life.

Having a postpartum depressed mother also could be a form of stress for the baby. Depressed mothers often are flat and unresponsive with their babies, which is upsetting for the infants and makes them cry. Their babies are less responsive to people, even to an adult who is trying to get them interested in an activity (Field et al. 1988). Postpartum depressed women seem clumsy and uncomfortable with their babies (Teti and Gelfand 1991). A woman who is depressed early in her child's life may have difficulty being a sensitive and responsive parent. Even if she provides for the baby's basic needs for food and safety, the way she relates to the baby could lead the child to form an insecure attachment bond, with negative consequences for the child later in life.

Early childhood stress can have a permanent impact on neurobiology such that these babies grow into children and adults who are highly reactive to stress.

Depressed Mothers' Relationships with Their Children

The third way that a mother's depression can have an impact on her children is through her relationship with them.

When we are depressed, we feel bad. We feel bad about ourselves and bad about the people we love. We're afraid they don't like us much, and we are constantly on the lookout for signs they will reject us. We feel hurt by unintentional slights. We have difficulty mustering the enthusiasm to engage with people.

A depressed woman also is preoccupied. She has difficulty concentrating because she is constantly pulled to thinking about what is bothering her.

Even when a depressed woman is not feeling sad, she may be irritable. Her temper is short. She has little tolerance for the noise and mess her children make. She may lack the patience to explain things to them or to listen while they talk. Literally, they get on her nerves. She may feel on the verge of screaming if they aren't quiet.

Researchers who have observed depressed women with their children see the impact of these symptoms on the mothers' behavior. Lovejoy and her colleagues (2000) reviewed these studies and came to the following conclusions.

First, depressed mothers have difficulty being positive and upbeat. They smile less and are less enthusiastic. They are less affectionate, and they don't praise their children as much as mothers usually do.

Second, depressed women seem preoccupied when they are with their children. They aren't really listening to what their kids are saying. They seem to be a million miles away, lost in their own thoughts. I saw one depressed woman put her two-month-old baby down on a chair then turn her back on the child to fill in a questionnaire. She became completely absorbed. When I glanced up from my desk a few seconds later, the baby was about to roll off the chair.

A mother who is not really paying attention cannot be consistent. Inconsistency is especially a problem when it comes to discipline. Behavior that is punished one time isn't noticed the next. Preoccupation may explain why depressed women often ignore their children's misbehavior until it gets so loud or intolerable that they are forced to act. This inconsistency is hard for children to cope with because they can't figure out what to do to get the response they want from their parents.

Third, depressed women often are angry with their kids and critical of them. One depressed woman told me her thirteen-year-old daughter was "weird" because she stayed in her room reading books. Another mother called her fourteen-year-old daughter a "slut" because she dressed in low-slung jeans and navel-baring tops. Even women who are not depressed currently but who have a history of depression are more negative and angry with their children than are other women. The depressed mother's hostility and criticism can make her children feel rejected and lead to insecure attachment.

Despite these difficulties, the kids of depressed moms aren't at particular risk for forming insecure attachments to their mothers. Some children do, but others don't. On average, a group of depressed women is less warm with their children than a group of women who are not depressed, but this doesn't mean that all depressed mothers are not warm or that they lack warmth all the time. Depressed mothers who are comfortable with close relationships and can stay connected to the people they love may have attachment bonds with their children that are more secure than do mothers whose depression leads them to withdraw and isolate themselves. In a recent study, I showed that kids are at risk for depressive symptoms only if their depressed mothers have turned down the volume on their attachment needs (Whiffen, Kerr, and Kallos-Lilly 2005). Turning down the volume on their own emotional needs may make them less sensitive and less responsive to their children's needs.

There is a saying in clinical psychology that parents don't have to be perfect; they only have to be "good enough." Most children are able to tolerate a wide range of parental behavior and still feel connected to and loved by their parents.

DOES PARENTING EXPLAIN CHILDREN'S RISK FOR EMOTIONAL PROBLEMS?

Many researchers have suggested that the way depressed women interact with their children explains their children's emotional distress.

This is largely an untested idea. The few studies that have been done support the idea that depressed women's relationships with their children can explain at least part of their children's emotional distress. In particular, depressed mothers can be angry, harsh, and coercive with their children, especially when they are disciplining them. These behaviors are related to the child feeling depressed and acting out by disobeying rules, lying, and talking back. This link is especially clear for the sons of depressed mothers (Conger, Patterson, and Ge 1995).

When boys are seen for treatment because they are disobedient and rude, their mothers often are depressed. At first, clinicians assumed the boys were acting out because their mothers didn't discipline them properly. Depressed mothers tend not to follow through with discipline. Once they decide a behavior is unacceptable and they tell their child to stop, they don't check back to make sure they were obeyed. If they aren't obeyed, they don't persist. Boys learn that their depressed mothers don't follow through, so they ignore them.

Clinicians thought that the way to help these boys was to treat their mothers' depression. However, when researchers looked at these mothers and sons more closely, they found that the boys acted out only in part because their mothers' discipline was inconsistent or lax (Snyder 1991). Other factors that were not looked at in the study were coming into play as well, although we do not know what those factors are at the present time.

THE CONTEXT OF WOMEN'S DEPRESSION

When we look at the big picture, we see that both the depressed mother and her children live lives filled with conflict and stress (Goodman and Gotlib 1999). The mother may be divorced from the children's father. In that case, often the family is struggling financially. Even if the parents are not separated or divorced, the couple may have significant relationship problems. Families in which the mother is depressed lack intimacy and cohesion. Family members feel disconnected from each other. They may share little of what they are thinking or feeling, and they rarely do activities together. When we take this context into account, it becomes clear that these associated problems are more strongly linked to children's emotional distress than is the mother's depression in and of itself.

Davies and Windle (1997) found specific connections between types of family problems and adolescents' emotional well-being. Interestingly, these links differed for boys and girls.

The sons of depressed women are more likely to act out when the parents are divorced and the mother and her children are struggling financially. Under these circumstances, it may be difficult for women to be consistent disciplinarians with their sons. Financial problems may mean the mother has to go out to work, and she may have to leave her children unattended for long periods of time. When she returns from work, she may be tired, irritable, and impatient, so more likely to react harshly when her son misbehaves.

One divorced woman started work before her twelve-year-old son had to go to school. It was only after several months that she learned he often stayed home and played video games all day. He covered up his deception by forging her signature on sick notes for the school. When this mother found out how her son had been deceiving her, she was extremely upset and she punished him severely. However, within a few days she seemed to forget about what had happened, and things went back to normal.

The daughters of depressed women are more likely to act out when their family lacks intimacy. These parents may not know what their daughter is doing, which gives her the opportunity to get into trouble. However, insufficient supervision is unlikely to be the whole story. Children who lie, talk back, and disobey rules are angry with their parents. Being difficult and getting into trouble may be a way to connect, however negatively, with disengaged parents.

The daughters of depressed women are more likely to be depressed when their parents fight a lot. Fights create tension and stress for the whole family, not just the people directly involved. Parents who aren't getting along find it difficult to do family activities together. The family may split up, with each parent doing activities separately with children. Often this split forms along gender lines, with the mothers taking their daughters and the fathers taking their sons.

No one is sure why daughters are more affected by their parents' conflict than sons are. One possibility is that the daughter in this situation is drawn into a close relationship with her depressed mother. We know that just being close to someone who is depressed infects our mood (Joiner and Katz 1999). In some cases, these girls seem to feel responsible for their parents' marital problems. One daughter felt she had to be constantly aware of what was happening between her parents so she could head off their fights. She would try to change their mood by joking with them or to separate them by drawing one of her parents away. Although she probably forestalled a number of their fights, she couldn't stop them all. When the inevitable happened, she felt as if she had failed. Feeling responsible for something that is completely out of our control can make us feel depressed.

THE PLACE OF THE FATHER

The philosopher Bertrand Russell joked that the place of the father in the modern suburban family is a very small one—particularly if he plays golf.

Fathers are thought to be insignificant figures in modern families. For the longest time, research psychologists thought they were important only if they were absent, so fathers were studied only in the context of divorce. For the past ten years, this view of fathers has begun to change, and psychologists now accept that fathers are an important part of the family context.

As I discussed in chapter 8, women who are prone to depression seem to be drawn to men who are cold, distant, reserved, and unsupportive. These men are unresponsive as romantic partners, and they also may have trouble being warm, responsive parents to their children and stepchildren.

Nearly half of the men who live with depressed women have emotional problems (Merikangas et al. 1988). Depressed women are particularly likely to have relationships with men who use alcohol or drugs excessively. One study of Australian teenagers found that the combination of a depressed mother and an alcoholic or drug-abusing father figure was strongly associated with depression in their adolescent children (Brennan et al. 2002). These families were highly stressed. Maybe they had financial problems because of the man's drinking or drug use. The stress also could have been interpersonal. Conflict between people is much more likely when one or both have been drinking. These fathers and stepfathers were very critical of the adolescent children in their families. They spoke about them in demeaning terms and were quick to point out their inadequacies. These two factors—family stress and having a critical male parent—accounted for the adolescents' depression in these families.

Suzanne and Bob

Suzanne was a forty-year-old woman married to a man named Bob. They had two young sons, Sam and Daniel, and a seventeen-year-old son named Dylan. In our first session, Suzanne told me she had been depressed for several years because of her relationship with Bob, who she described as angry, domineering, and critical of her and the children. To cope with Bob's anger, she made herself "as small as possible" by trying to stay out of his way and be pleasant. This strategy stabilized their relationship, which she felt she had learned to tolerate.

However, Bob's anger had an impact on all three sons. Daniel was anxious and doing poorly at school. Sam was angry and rebellious. He had no friends and was described by his teachers as "disruptive." Dylan was a "nervous" child who had many emotional problems and was struggling to finish high school.

Suzanne seemed to have good relationships with her children and a good idea of what they needed from her as a parent. The one difficulty she noted was that she had trouble disciplining the boys. She felt they often took advantage of her. For instance, they wouldn't clean up after themselves because they knew if they left a mess she would eventually pick it up. She had a hard time being firm with the boys because she felt Bob was overly strict. She tried to give the boys a break when they were alone with her and "let them be children." When Bob worked late, she fed them pizza and other food Bob did not allow, and she let them come into her bedroom and lie on the bed watching TV in their pajamas.

Suzanne said Bob had experienced many disappointments at work. To cope, he drank. Often he would start as soon as he got home, and by dinnertime he would be drunk. The more he drank, the more critical he was of Dylan. As the family sat around the dinner table, he would cross-examine Dylan about what he had learned at school that day and ridicule the boy's halting attempts to tell him. He would tell Dylan that he was "stupid" and would never amount to anything. When I asked Suzanne what she did during these dinners, she told me she always made sure to sit beside Dylan so she could take his hand beneath the table and squeeze his fingers. This was the only way she felt she could support him without having a fight with Bob.

All of Suzanne's children had emotional problems. Although her relationships with them were warm, she had trouble with discipline, particularly with following through when she asked them to do something. Her disciplinary style probably contributed to Sam's disobedience because she did not provide him with clear rules about what was and wasn't acceptable behavior. She thought she was compensating for Bob's severity with the children, but she wasn't really doing Sam a favor. The kids at school rejected Sam because he didn't know how to behave appropriately. Suzanne also undermined Bob's relationships with his sons. By being lenient when Bob was not at home, she communicated that she thought Bob's rules were unfair. When parents are unhappily married, it's not uncommon for one parent to align with the children against the other.

When we look at the family context, we can see that Suzanne's depression played a small part in the difficulties her sons experienced. The family was stressed by Bob and Suzanne's unhappy marriage and by Bob's work problems, his drinking, and his anger. Bob's criticism of Dylan was explicit and likely contributed to Dylan's nervousness. Bob's anger also seems to have been a factor in Sam's anger and Daniel's anxiety. Both boys were afraid of their dad, but Sam rebelled while Daniel shrank in fear. It was the whole family context that was distressing for the children, not just their mother's depression.

HELPING THE CHILD OF A DEPRESSED MOTHER

You can help your child develop skills that will protect her against depression in the future. A child who is easily upset, who has difficulty calming down, or who is fearful and withdrawn may have inherited some of the genetic risk. The following strategies are good for all children but particularly for those at risk.

Emotion Coaching

Children need help managing negative feelings like anger and sadness. Younger children often don't know what they're feeling, and they can't connect their feelings to events that may have triggered those feelings.

Parents differ in the ways they handle children's negative feelings. Some parents are dismissive of children's emotions. They see negative feelings as potentially harmful to children. They think it's their job to change the child's bad feelings as quickly as possible. They may tell the child that bad feelings are unimportant and will pass. They may encourage their children to "ride out" bad feelings or tell them to suppress them. Or they may deny or ignore bad feelings.

Other parents are aware and accepting of emotions. They know what they're feeling, and they can tell or guess what their child might be feeling. They see negative emotions as an opportunity. Talking about feelings is a chance to get closer to the child and to understand her better. When the child feels bad, there is an opportunity to teach her how to use emotions to solve problems. These parents *validate* what the child is feeling. That is, they accept the child's feelings and try to understand them from the child's point of view, even if the child's emotional response is very different from their own. They help the child label her emotions. Labeling allows children to differentiate among feelings. For instance, a feeling of loneliness is more specific than a feeling of sadness. When we are better able to differentiate our feelings, we are better able to figure out where they come from. Once the child can express what she is feeling, the parent helps her to identify the situation that caused the feeling and to problem-solve about how to improve it. John Gottman calls these parental behaviors *emotion coaching* (Gottman, Katz, and Hooven 1996).

Emotion coaching benefits children in three ways. First, a parent who is an emotion coach is less likely to put a child down. A parent who derogates a child is critical, mocks her, or blames her when things go wrong. Parents who behave this way toward their children communicate rejection.

Second, parents who emotion coach are more likely to actively help their children solve problems. Problem solving is a good coping strategy that helps prevent depression.

Third, when parents are emotion coaches, their children are less biologically responsive to stress and better able to calm themselves down when they do get upset. This is a fascinating finding. Some researchers believe that just talking over a problem is soothing for children.

We don't know whether emotion coaching prevents children from becoming depressed. However, Gottman and his colleagues showed that children who are emotion coached have better relationships with other kids and do better at school. Having good friendships and doing well at school enhance a child's self-esteem, which is protective against depression.

Feelings of anger and sadness may be difficult for a depressed woman to talk about. Because she has experienced firsthand the intense sadness that goes along with depression, she may want to protect her children from having these feelings. She even may feel her child's sadness as keenly as she feels her own.

It's important to remember that your experience of sadness may be much more painful than your child's experience. As much as you want to protect your child from feeling bad, if you dismiss or deny her sadness, she may be at greater risk than she would have been if you had talked with her about her feelings.

A depressed woman also may have problems with anger. Although she may get irritable and angry herself, she is likely to be sensitive to this emotion in others and quick to believe their anger is directed at her. Again, her own discomfort with anger may make her want to get rid of the feeling as quickly as possible.

The toughest situation for a parent occurs when a child is angry or sad about something the parent has done. Even in the best relationships, this happens. Most parents want these feelings to go away quickly because they make parents uncomfortable. We can interpret anger as a challenge to our authority and see sadness as feedback that we're not a good enough parent. However, this is exactly the situation in which it is important for us to put aside our emotions and try to coach our children to label and understand theirs.

Not that long ago, my son, who is usually a cheerful fourteen-year-old, was obviously upset. He got quiet and sullen. Although I asked what was wrong several times, he told me he was fine. After a couple of days, my husband took him out alone and asked what was wrong. My son explained that he had put a lot of effort into cleaning up our garage in anticipation of some relatives visiting. I had asked him to do this task, but I hadn't thanked him for his efforts. He felt hurt and unappreciated. My husband could have told our son not to be silly. After all, we had all done a lot to get ready, and my son knew he was expected to help. Instead, my husband validated our son's feelings. Then he told me what had happened. I felt bad that my son's feelings were hurt, but my initial thought was to point out to him that no one had thanked me for the cleaning and cooking I had done. Like a lot of parents, I didn't like the idea that I'd done something to upset him, and I wanted him not to feel that way. Then I remembered that you can't talk people out of the way they feel. In any case, my son was right to feel unappreciated. I was so busy getting ready for the visit that I hadn't even looked at all the work he'd done cleaning up the garage. I apologized to him; he gave me a big smile and a hug, and we were back to normal.

I wish I could say it's always this easy. What helped in this case was that my husband was able to get our son talking about his feelings. Sometimes children find it easier to have a conversation about emotions with the parent they aren't hurt or angry with. It also helped that I trusted my husband to give me constructive feedback. When couples are fighting or insecurely attached to each other, this kind of feedback can easily be taken as criticism.

Seeking Support

Children should be encouraged to seek emotional support when they're upset. The best way to do this is by listening to the child and *validating* what she is feeling. Validating a child's feelings does not mean agreeing with her; it means understanding from her point of view what she is feeling and why. A child who feels understood is learning that people will listen to her when she's upset.

Children who are shy, fearful, and withdrawn are at risk for developing insecure attachment bonds. Parents may need to be particularly sensitive and responsive to these children's emotional needs.

While relationships with parents are very important for preschool-aged children, relationships with other kids become increasingly important as children mature. Shy and fearful children can benefit from out-of-home day care (Bohlin, Hagekull, and Andersson 2005). If they are looked after at home by family members, they may not get enough contact with other kids. When they go to school, lack of experience can cause them to be awkward socially, which leads to them being ignored or even rejected by other children. Failure in a social situation makes children feel extremely anxious and may cause a shy child to withdraw further. Out-of-home day care provides these children with the chance to play with other children and to develop their social skills. Good social skills will help them get the support they need from friends later in life.

Learned Optimism

An *optimist* is a person who always finds a way to see the glass as half full. Even in a bad situation, the optimist can see something that is good. She has confidence that a situation that doesn't look good at first can change and ultimately turn out all right. Optimism is the belief that things will get better in the future. The optimist doesn't deny reality. As one research psychologist put it, "When there is room for doubt, [the optimist] fills the gap with hope" (Peterson 2000, 51). Optimists live in a world where their hopes come true. When Peterson reviewed the research literature, he found that optimists are happier, physically healthier, and better able to accomplish their goals than pessimists.

Some children are natural optimists. The children's story *Pollyanna* is about a girl who is able to see the good in people and in situations that would discourage most of us. Whether a child is an optimist probably depends in part on her temperament. A child who experiences a lot of negative emotion is probably not inclined to be an optimist. The attitudes that her parents model for her also are important. Children watch their parents and imitate what they see, particularly if the parent is the same sex as the child.

Children can be taught to be optimistic. Lisa Jaycox chose a group of kids at risk for depression in part because they already felt down and in part because their parents fought a lot (Jaycox et al. 1994). She wanted to teach these children how to cope with negative events so they wouldn't get more depressed. She taught them how to recognize when they were thinking pessimistically about a situation. She taught them to challenge their pessimistic thoughts and to replace them with thoughts that were more hopeful.

Jaycox tested the kids before and after she taught them to be optimistic as well as six months and two years later. She found that teaching kids to be more optimistic not only reduced the amount of depression they felt at the time but also stopped them from getting depressed later. Even two years later, they were only half as likely to be depressed as high-risk kids who had not had her training (Gillham et al. 1995).

The key ingredient in Jaycox's training was the way children explained negative events. Children who learned to see negative events as being due to unstable causes were less likely to become depressed. Take as an example a child doing poorly on a math test. A *stable* explanation would be that she can't do math. If she can't do math, she won't do any better on future tests. This conclusion is demoralizing. In contrast, an *unstable* explanation would be that she didn't study enough for this test. If she believes the cause of her poor performance was some temporary factor, she will be less demoralized and more motivated to figure out how she can do better the next time.

Changing how a child thinks about the causes of negative events may seem like a small thing. However, Jaycox found that the children who became more optimistic were better able to solve problems, especially interpersonal ones, and better able to handle conflict.

As a woman who has experienced depression, you may have trouble teaching your children to be optimistic. Pessimism is part of your life experience. Perhaps your pessimism can be justified by many experiences of disappointment and loss. It's important for you to realize that your children's experiences may not be the same as yours. Teaching children to become optimistic may require you to set aside your own automatic conclusions when bad things happen.

One depressed mother had a thirteen-year-old daughter named Cynthia. One of Cynthia's friends was turning fourteen, and the day before her birthday she called Cynthia to invite her to a party. Cynthia accepted, but when she told her mother about the party, her mother insisted that inviting her was "just a gift grab." The mother explained that if the girl really wanted Cynthia to come to her party, she would have invited her sooner. She made Cynthia call her friend back and say she couldn't come. When Cynthia got to school on Monday morning, she learned that all of the other kids in the class had been at the birthday party. Her friend's parents had allowed her to have a mixed party at the last minute. Not only had Cynthia missed her friend's birthday, but she also had missed the first mixed party in her class.

I certainly understood why Cynthia's mother was suspicious of the last-minute invitation. However, her mother assumed that the birthday girl didn't really like her daughter and only asked her to the party to get a gift. That is, she assumed a stable and negative cause for the last-minute invitation. The mother allowed her own pessimism about relationships to shape the way she advised her daughter to handle the situation.

If the mother had been more aware of this tendency in herself, she could have handled the situation differently. For instance, she could have called the girl's parents to get more information. She would have quickly learned that it was being pulled together at the last minute. Or she could have talked to her daughter about how things had been going with the birthday girl. Was there any reason to think the birthday girl didn't really like Cynthia? The mother could have found out if Cynthia cared whether the invitation was late. Children are much less sensitive to social niceties than adults are. If Cynthia didn't care, there really wasn't any reason to stop her from going.

When we think about bad things having stable causes, we get locked into a particular way of seeing them. When we consider the possibility of an unstable cause, we can generate alternative explanations.

LIKE MOTHER, LIKE CHILD? NOT NECESSARILY

The children of depressed mothers are at risk for a variety of problems. In part, this risk stems from the negative impact depression may have on women's relationships with their children, particularly when it comes to discipline. However, a woman's depression usually occurs in a context that may be more harmful to her children than her depression in and of itself. One important way a woman can protect her children is by improving the context in which they live. She also can help her children build skills that will protect them from becoming depressed later. Helping children to understand and use their emotions to solve interpersonal problems, helping them to turn to other people for support, and teaching them to be more optimistic are all strategies that can reduce children's risk.

Questions to Ask Yourself

1. Do I worry that my child is at risk for depression? Why? Did what I read in this chapter reassure me or confirm my fears?

2. Does my child seem to have emotional problems? Does she act out? Does she seem anxious or sad? Does she have good friends? How does she feel about herself? How well is she doing in school? Are there activities she's really good at?

3. Does my child seem to have the genetic risk for depression? Has she always been anxious? Has she always been shy? Is she easily upset and hard to soothe?

4. Was I stressed while I was pregnant with her? Did I experience postpartum depression?

5. When I feel down, is it hard to be positive with my child? Do I get angry with her a lot? Do I criticize her and put her down? Do I sometimes find that I'm not really paying attention to what she's saying or doing? Is it an effort to discipline her? Does she seem to be insecurely attached to me? If so, has she turned the volume up or down?

6. Is there a lot of stress in our life? Am I worried about money or my relationships with friends, relatives, or coworkers? Are there other things I'm stressed about? Does my partner's drinking or use of drugs cause problems? Is my partner mean to my child? Do people in our family fight a lot? How often do we do fun things together? How often do we laugh together? Do I know what's going on in my child's life? Do I encourage her to talk to me?

7. Do I sometimes tell my child too much about what's happening with me? Does she seem to feel responsible for making me feel better?

8. Can I think of a time recently that my child obviously felt sad or angry? What did I do? Did I dismiss her feelings or try to make them go away? Did I talk to her about them? Did I validate what she was feeling? Did I try to help her solve whatever problem made her feel bad?

9. Can I think of a time recently that something bad happened to my child? What did I do? How did I talk to her about the bad event? Did I try to think of a number of reasons why it might have happened? Did I jump to conclusions about what had happened? Did my child feel better or worse after talking about it with me?

CHAPTER 10

our lives don't change, we change: treatment options

By now you probably have a good idea why you experience depression, and your question is "What can I do about it?" You could do nothing at all. If you have never been depressed before and the life stress that triggered your depression is time limited, you could become well again without treatment. However, if you have had previous experiences with depression or the stress in your life is ongoing, you may need help. Fortunately, there are good treatments for women who are depressed. Steve Hollon and other depression researchers surveyed the research comparing the various treatment options (Hollon et al. 2005). I discuss their findings in this chapter so you can make the best choice for you.

YOUR TREATMENT OPTIONS

Hollon and his colleagues (2005) reported that one of out every four depressive episodes ends without the person getting any treatment at all. Untreated episodes last on average nine months. Most likely, these episodes end because the stress that triggered the depression ends. For instance, a woman might feel depressed right after ending a romantic relationship but feel better as times goes on. If this woman has never been depressed before, if she is not severely depressed now, and if she has not had repeated experiences with the kinds of interpersonal problems I've talked about in this book, her depression is likely to get better on its own. While she might find therapy or counseling useful at this time in her life, she probably does not need any form of treatment to stop feeling depressed.

The more chronic or complicated a woman's history of depression, the less likely she is to get better without professional help. A woman who has been depressed often or for longer periods of time or who has had many difficult interpersonal relationships would be wise to consider the treatment options that are available to her.

ANTIDEPRESSANT MEDICATION

Most women who go to a family doctor for treatment are prescribed antidepressant medication. There are three major types of antidepressants: monoamine oxidase inhibitors (MAOIs), tricyclics (for example, imipramine), and selective serotonin reuptake inhibitors (SSRIs, for example, Prozac).

Most media attention, both for and against the use of drugs, has focused on the SSRIs. However, hundreds of studies have shown that all classes of antidepressants are equally effective. One out of every two women who take an antidepressant at the prescribed dose for the recommended time will stop feeling depressed. SSRIs are usually prescribed before other antidepressants because they have less severe side effects.

All antidepressants are more effective than a *placebo*. A placebo is a pill that lacks active ingredients but which is taken regularly by the patient as if it were real medication. In research, the study participant doesn't know if she is receiving the active drug or the placebo. Placebos measure the effect that simply taking a pill has on symptoms. About a quarter of the women who are given placebos get better, possibly because their depression would have improved without treatment.

The biggest advantage of antidepressants is that they work quickly. Most women notice improvement within four weeks. Different antidepressants have different biochemical effects. If a woman's depression has not improved within eight weeks, the American Psychiatric Association (APA) recommends changing to a different class of antidepressant. If there has been partial improvement, the APA recommends adding another antidepressant to the one the patient is already taking, a strategy that often works.

Half of the people who experience an episode of depression have another episode at a later time in their lives. The risk of relapse increases with every episode of depression experienced (Belsher and Costello 1988). So one important feature of treatment is whether it protects against future episodes.

The APA recommends that patients take antidepressants for up to a year after their symptoms improve to prevent another episode. Women who have responded to the drug are protected from becoming depressed again as long as they take the drug. Once they stop, they are at risk. Women who have experienced many episodes of severe depression may decide to take antidepressants for the rest of their lives. At this time, we do not know whether the lifetime use of antidepressants is a health risk.

Many people do not want to take antidepressants. Some worry they will become addicted. Others fear that antidepressants do not really solve their problems. The side effects can be significant. They can include sexual problems, insomnia, weight gain, and a feeling of emotional detachment or blunting. In clinical trials, about 15 percent of people stop taking their medication because of the side effects. For all these reasons, some people stop taking the drug as prescribed. They skip days, take only part of the recommended dose, or stop altogether. When people don't take the medication as prescribed, it is not helpful.

PSYCHOTHERAPY

There are more than 200 kinds of psychotherapy, but most of them have not been proven to be effective as treatments for emotional distress. In the following sections, I describe the four types of psychotherapy that researchers have shown to be effective for treating depression. Three of these are called *individual* therapies because they involve treating only the depressed woman, while the fourth involves the depressed woman and her spouse or romantic partner. All of these psychotherapies treat depression as effectively as antidepressant medication. Again, about half of depressed women get better with psychotherapy. In addition, each kind of therapy has specific benefits, and there is new evidence that each one is best suited to a different kind of person or problem.

Interpersonal Therapy

THE THEORY BEHIND THE THERAPY

Interpersonal therapy (IPT) was developed by Gerald Klerman and his colleagues, who had extensive experience as researchers of depression (Klerman et al. 1984). Treatment usually takes twelve to sixteen one-hour sessions. The goals are to reduce depressive symptoms and improve interpersonal relationships.

IPT therapists do not assume that a specific episode of depression was caused by relationship problems. However, they believe that improving relationships reduces depressive symptoms. Because the theory is rooted in Bowlby's ideas about attachment, as described in chapter 5, IPT therapists recognize that childhood relationships have an impact on how we feel and what we do in adult relationships. However, therapy normally focuses on present relationships rather than past ones.

IPT assumes that depression is linked to problems in one of four domains.

Depression can be linked to a *role transition*. A role transition happens when a major life event occurs that results in the person taking on a new role. Having a baby is a common example. New mothers have to get used to the considerable demands of caring for a baby and leave behind whatever parts of their old self they have lost, such as "working woman," "slim and physically fit," or even "no ties or responsibilities." When a role transition has occurred, the goal is to help the depressed woman mourn the loss of the old role and feel capable in her new one. An IPT therapist would help a postpartum depressed woman develop her competence as a mother while mourning whatever losses she has experienced.

Interpersonal disputes occur when a depressed woman is in conflict with someone who is important to her: her spouse or romantic partner, her parents or another family member, or her boss or coworkers. Role transitions often lead to interpersonal disputes because our lives change faster than our relationships.

Tracy had interpersonal disputes with both her mother and Matt. Her problem with her mother involved Tracy's feeling that her mother didn't care for her. Her conflict with Matt focused on housework and child care. Like some new fathers, Matt believed his life did not need to change just because he was a father. He thought Tracy could take care of the housework because she wasn't working outside their home. The goal of IPT in a case like this is either to resolve the dispute by changing the behavior of the people involved or their expectations of one another, or to end the relationship and mourn its loss. An IPT therapist would help Tracy to negotiate Matt's greater involvement in housework, to lower her expectations of him, or to end the relationship if he did not want to change.

IPT therapists see *unresolved grief and loss* as another problem area related to depression. Loss is a normal part of life. With time, people are usually able to accept losses and move on. However, losses can lead to depression, particularly when they are unexpected and unwanted. When people get stuck in their grief, they are said to be *unresolved*.

Anne experienced unresolved grief when Bill left her. Although she was unhappy in the marriage, she wasn't able to accept the loss and move on because she had paid such a high price to keep Bill in her life. Giving up on him meant admitting that her sacrifices had been in vain. The goal of IPT in a case like this is to help the depressed woman process the loss emotionally and develop new relationships to fill the void left by the person who was lost. An IPT therapist would help Anne mourn the loss of her marriage and become involved in new activities and relationships.

The category of *interpersonal deficits* is used when a specific life event did not precede the depressive episode. In this case, IPT focuses on depressed persons' social isolation. We all need to feel connected to our communities and to the people whose lives we share. IPT therapists believe that people who lack close friends and who feel lonely and isolated are not only at risk for depression but are unlikely to make a full recovery without some improvement in their social relationships. The goal of therapy in this case is to help the client build closer, more supportive relationships.

At the beginning of IPT, the therapist identifies one or two problem areas that are related to the client's depression. This problem area becomes the focus of therapy. Individual sessions involve the client and therapist talking about difficulties that the client has experienced in her problem area since their last session. Together, they try to figure out what the client wanted in an interpersonal situation and what went wrong. They try to figure out how the situation could be handled differently in the future, and they may role-play different possibilities so the client has a chance to practice doing things differently.

IPT WORKS

Hollon and his colleagues (2005) reviewed the research on the effectiveness of IPT. Several studies have shown that IPT is just as effective as antidepressants in the treatment of depression. Half of the women who receive IPT are no longer depressed at the end of treatment. It takes longer for a woman who is receiving IPT to notice she is feeling better than for a woman who is taking antidepressants, but the improvement is just as great in the end.

Therapy can continue after the depression has improved to prevent the woman from becoming depressed again. Women who continue with IPT are protected from having another episode but not as well-protected as women who continue to take antidepressants.

Within a year, women who receive IPT notice improvement in their relationships. This is a specific effect that is not found with antidepressants. The women who do best in IPT are those who have more satisfying relationships at the beginning of therapy. These women likely value relationships and believe that having good relationships can make them happier.

TRACY: *CHANGED EXPECTATIONS*

IPT was a good choice for Tracy. When I first met her, she had been depressed for eighteen months. Like half of the women prescribed antidepressants, her depression did not respond to various medications, either alone or in combination. She was severely depressed. I saw her for eighteen sessions over a ten-month period. For financial reasons, we had six weekly sessions followed by several monthly sessions with another cluster of seven weekly sessions near the end of treatment. Consistent with the research on IPT, her depressive symptoms did not disappear completely until late in therapy. By this time, her social relationships had improved considerably.

Although Tracy had experienced a role transition before becoming depressed, her depression was not related to being a new mother. Instead, she was in conflict with two key people in her life: her mother and her partner.

As I described in chapter 6, our early sessions focused on Tracy's relationship with her mother. Tracy wanted her mother to admit she had neglected her daughters. She wanted to tell her mother how she felt, and she wanted to understand why her mother had made the choices she had. However, when Tracy had this conversation, her mother told her that she had no cause for complaint because she had not been sexually abused as her sister had been.

The goal of IPT when there is an interpersonal dispute is to either resolve the dispute or help the client end the relationship. In my clinical experience, ending a relationship with a parent is rarely an option. Tracy did not end her relationship with her mother. However, she did change her attitude toward it. She accepted that her mother cared "minimally" for her, but instead of blaming herself for not being a good enough daughter, she told herself that her mother had been too young and inexperienced to be a good mother.

Tracy's change in attitude led to an important change in her behavior. She stopped trying to win her mother's love, for instance, by loaning her money and solving her problems. Interestingly, this change did not lead to greater distance between them. By the end of therapy, Tracy told me she felt less exploited by her mother and as a result, better able to relax and joke around with her. Their relationship was better than it had ever been.

The new relationships Tracy formed after starting therapy also were much better. Tracy told me she was different with her new friends. She was more self-confident and more certain that she deserved to be treated well. As a result, she felt more accepted and better cared for by them.

It was interesting to me that Tracy initially denied having problems with Matt. It was only as she explored her relationship with her mother that she was able to admit having similar feelings about Matt. In my clinical work, this often happens. A woman will start by talking about a relationship that is less important to her, and as her feelings in it are understood, she will move on to talking about a more significant relationship.

IPT worked well for Tracy because the therapy matched her beliefs about why she had become depressed. From our first session, she described herself as someone who placed a lot of importance on relationships and who felt comfortable being close to people. Although as a child she had learned to turn down the volume with regard to her emotional needs and to depend only on herself, she yearned for a relationship in which she could feel close, comfortable, trusting, and safe.

Cognitive Behavioral Therapy

THE THEORY BEHIND THE THERAPY

Cognitive behavioral therapy (CBT) was developed by Aaron T. Beck and his colleagues (Beck et al. 1979). As described in chapter 1, Beck's central idea is that depressed people see themselves, their world, and their future in a negative light. These negative beliefs are not necessarily accurate. Often they are *cognitive distortions*—biases in the way depressed people think. Whether they are true or not, they have a powerful impact on how we feel. When something bad happens, a person who is prone to depression interprets the event through the lens of their negative beliefs and they feel depressed. Beck was the first clinician to link what we think to how we feel.

Later, he came to believe that negative beliefs and cognitive distortions are the result of *cognitive schemas* (Beck 1983). Schemas are consistent ways of thinking that are evident across situations. For instance, many people who are prone to depression think it is important to have other people's approval. If others don't approve of them, these depressed people feel they must be deficient. People with a high need for approval seek it in many situations and with many people, even with people they don't know well or don't like.

The need for approval is so strong that it overrides other ways a depressed person might see a situation. One depressed woman turned down a promotion at work because she did not want to risk being rejected by the other women in her office. The promotion would have made her a boss. She and the other women made fun of the bosses. She put her workmates' approval ahead of her own need to advance and make more money. According to Beck, the person with a high need for approval is at risk for depression when a negative interpersonal event happens. For instance, people with this cognitive schema are thought to be at risk for depression when a romantic relationship ends.

Beck considers the need for approval to be one of two cognitive schemas that are associated with depression. The other schema is the need for autonomy. People with a high need for autonomy want to be independent of other people and not be controlled by them. They put a premium on work and achievement rather than relationships, so they are prone to depression when they fail to reach an important life goal. For instance, an autonomous person who fails out of school or is fired from her job would be at risk for depression. Women with a high need for autonomy also may be at risk for postpartum depression because having a baby entails a loss of personal control.

Beck believes that cognitive schemas develop as a result of early learning experiences. For instance, Lisa had a high need for approval. This makes sense when we consider that her parents were very demanding and punished her severely when she didn't meet their expectations. Tracy had a high need for autonomy. She had been neglected by her mother, so she learned to rely on herself. In fact, it felt dangerous to place her welfare in another person's hands.

Many people who experience depression have both cognitive schemas. This can create tension between their needs to please others and to be self-reliant. They can behave in ways that are contradictory and confusing to other people.

WHAT HAPPENS IN CBT?

Treatment with CBT has three distinct parts. At the beginning, the goal is to get depressed people active again. Clients are asked to keep lists of the activities they do every day along with ratings of how much fun they had and how capable they felt while doing the activity. Based on these records, the CBT therapist assigns the client increasingly difficult activities that will make them feel happy and more self-confident. Clients may discuss these new activities in detail with the therapist before doing them so they can anticipate problems.

Anne enjoyed taking long walks. A CBT therapist would note from her record of daily activities that she enjoyed walking and that walks lifted her mood. To make walking more challenging, the therapist might assign Anne longer or more frequent walks or ask her to invite along the friend with whom she used to walk regularly. Anne might object that she couldn't invite her friend because she was too depressed to talk, to which the CBT therapist might reply that she could warn her friend that she might not feel like talking.

In the second phase of therapy, the goal is to challenge the client's cognitive distortions. The CBT therapist listens for times that the client sees a situation negatively and feels sad or acts in a depressed way, for instance by going to bed early. These are times that the client's cognitive distortions may have been operating. Another way of identifying cognitive distortions is through a daily record. The client notes times during the day that she felt bad and describes what happened just before she felt bad and what thoughts she had at that time. In therapy sessions, the therapist and client go over the daily record to connect negative thoughts to depressed feelings and to see if the negative thoughts were justified. If the negative thoughts were not justified, the CBT therapist challenges them. The therapist also may take this opportunity to talk about what the client could have done differently.

Anne often worried she would die an "impoverished old woman." A CBT therapist would see these thoughts as cognitive distortions because Anne had a substantial nest egg from her years with Bill. Anne was less concerned about having no money than about being alone. A CBT therapist would point out that whenever Anne imagined being old and alone, she felt sad and lonely. She felt bad about something that hadn't even happened yet. Then the therapist would pose a series of questions to challenge the validity of her belief that she would end up alone. What evidence did Anne have that she would always be alone? Didn't she have lots of friends? Didn't she have a good relationship with her sister? Anne would have clarified that she was afraid of never being loved by a man. The CBT therapist would ask if she had tried to meet a man since separating from Bill. Learning that she had not, the therapist might suggest that Anne needed more evidence to test the truth of her assumption.

In the third phase of CBT, the therapist tries to change the client's cognitive schemas. By listening to the systematic ways that her thinking is distorted, the therapist can see which of the typical cognitive schemas is operating. The therapist brings the schema to her attention and invites her to discuss it. Does her schema have some advantages as well as disadvantages? Does it have short-term advantages but long-term disadvantages? The therapist may assign the client homework so they both can see when her schema is operating. The therapist challenges the validity of the client's schema in the same way she/he challenged the client's cognitive distortions.

Anne had a high need for approval. While married, she was very concerned with Bill's opinion of her, and she made numerous changes in an attempt to please him. As predicted by Beck's theory, her depression followed the end of their marriage. Leaving her was Bill's ultimate statement of disapproval. Even Anne's fears about being old and penniless were not so much fears about money as fears she would end up isolated and unloved. A CBT therapist would get Anne to talk about her belief that she could not be happy unless she pleased others. Trying to please Bill was useful during their marriage because he was a harsh critic. However, is it useful or even possible to have everyone's approval, all of the time? The therapist would challenge the idea that Anne could not enjoy life without an approving husband by pointing out times she felt happy and content acting in the theater and socializing with her friends.

CBT WORKS

Hollon and his colleagues (2005) also reviewed the research assessing the effectiveness of CBT. Generally, CBT is as effective as both antidepressants and IPT in treating depression. However, CBT may be less effective than the other treatments if the person is severely depressed, especially if the CBT therapist is not very experienced.

Women who are successfully treated with CBT are at reduced risk for depression over the following two years. This is a specific effect that is not seen with other treatments. Of women who are successfully treated with antidepressants, 50 to 80 percent will become depressed again once they stop taking their medication. Among women successfully treated with CBT, this risk is halved. CBT may teach women ways to combat the negative thinking that spirals down into depression.

The women who do best with CBT are those who prefer some emotional distance in their relationships. Clients in CBT do not develop an intimate relationship with their therapist. In fact, CBT therapists are encouraged to be collaborators rather than confidantes. The CBT therapist sees him- or herself as someone who works with the client as an equal. This stance may not fit some clients' expectations of a therapist.

Clients who do well in CBT also are not highly prone to cognitive distortions at the beginning of therapy. CBT therapists look at the evidence for the client's beliefs and challenge her when these beliefs are not supported. Women who are logical and who are persuaded by logical argument may be more likely to benefit from this approach.

Process-Experiential Therapy

THE THEORY BEHIND THE THERAPY

Another promising individual therapy for depression is called process-experiential therapy (PET) (Greenberg, Rice, and Elliott 1993). PET focuses on helping clients clarify and process their emotions. Often clients come to therapy aware that they feel bad but unable to specify what kind of bad. They seem confused when I ask: Is the feeling one of sadness or loneliness? Do they feel disappointed or that they have failed? Clarifying what clients are feeling is a powerful way of directing their attention to what is most important about their response to a negative situation or event.

Once a client's feelings are clarified, she and the therapist can begin to *process* the emotion. When we process an emotion, we allow it to unfold completely without censoring or judging it. In our culture, we put a lot of emphasis on emotional self-control. People can feel ashamed if they lose control, for instance, by laughing too loudly, crying in public, or expressing strong anger. Our cultural bias toward self-control can result in people cutting off certain uncomfortable emotions, such as sadness. When we cut off our feelings, we are not fully aware of the impact people and events have on us. This strategy can be adaptive if we have to stay in a painful situation. However, it stops us from fully appreciating the pain we feel in situations we can change.

Sometimes PET therapists use specific techniques to help people become aware of and process their emotions. For instance, in the *empty chair* technique, the client role-plays talking to an important person with whom she is in conflict. The goal is to help the client put into words complex and painful feelings and, potentially, to find a solution to the problem.

Often empty chair is used to help the client talk to a person who is no longer in her life. In chapter 8, I described using the empty chair technique with Anne to help her express her anger toward Bill. It was through this technique that I learned their marriage had never been consummated. Anne had withheld this information from me for many sessions, but it came out in her "conversation" with Bill. Clients often reveal things about themselves in these imagined conversations that weren't obvious when they talked to me about the relationship.

The *two chair* technique is used when a client experiences internal conflict. Part of her feels one way and part another. Internal conflict may be the reason a client is confused or unable to make a decision. In the two chair technique, the client takes one position while sitting in one of the chairs. From this chair, she fully expresses the feelings that are associated with that position. Once she has finished, she switches chairs and puts into words the alternative position. Often one of the positions sounds weak or hollow when the client puts it into words. This is the position the client thinks she "should" take rather than the one she truly feels. The two chair technique helps a client clarify the feelings that underlie the two sides of the internal conflict and can help her identify which one corresponds to her true feelings. For instance, a PET therapist might have explored Anne's contradictory feelings whenever she moved. On the one hand, she felt sad and lonely for what she had lost, while on the other, she chastised herself for being "needy" and "dependent." Use of the two chair technique might have shown Anne that when she criticized herself by calling herself needy, she was repeating Bill's criticism of her.

PET WORKS

One study looked at the effectiveness of PET in treating depression (Watson et al. 2003). Depressed men and women were treated with sixteen weekly sessions of either CBT or PET. About half of the clients in both treatments experienced significant improvement in their depression. In addition, clients who were treated with PET felt that their relationships improved by the end of treatment. They felt more assertive, less accommodating and self-sacrificing, and less "needy" in relationships. This is a specific effect that is not found for CBT or antidepressants.

Studies have not been done to see what kind of client is better suited to PET than to other types of psychotherapy. However, we know that both IPT and CBT work better for clients who accept the basic assumptions of the therapy. I suspect PET works best for clients who value their emotions and who believe that knowing how they feel is an important part of making good choices.

LISA: *PET AS A TREATMENT FOR CHILDHOOD SEXUAL ABUSE*

PET was a good choice for Lisa. As a musician, she was exquisitely attuned to her inner life. She did not need techniques like empty chair to access and clarify her emotions. She knew what she was feeling and she suspected why. However, she had never told her story. Therapists who work with women who were sexually abused believe that these women need to tell their story to someone who cares (Herman 1992). In our early sessions, I helped Lisa clarify her feelings about her father, and I showed her that what had happened to her was important to me. From that point on, I was primarily a supportive and sympathetic listener.

Once Lisa fully appreciated the impact the abuse had on her, particularly on her intimate relationships, she turned her attention to her marriage. With the help of a couple therapist who also worked from a process-experiential perspective, Lisa and David were able to change their marriage so that it was more intimate and more satisfying for both of them.

Consistent with the research, working in a process-experiential way not only helped with Lisa's depression but also with her relationships. She did not end her relationship with her father. Like Tracy, Lisa changed it. Her relationship with her father was cool and distant by the time she finished therapy, and she told me he often complained he had "lost [his] little girl." However, she felt less controlled by him and more mature. This was probably the best resolution Lisa could hope for while keeping her father in her life.

She did develop a closer relationship with her younger sister. This sister had had an affair with David the year before Lisa started therapy. As Lisa got to know her sister, she realized they both had been abused by their father. This knowledge helped Lisa understand why her sister had had an affair with David, which allowed her to forgive them.

When therapy is successful, it not only helps the client feel better, it expands her world. Because the client is no longer consumed by painful feelings, she can turn her energy toward the world outside. Lisa developed a strong interest in children's welfare, which she channeled into setting up a system of high-quality and affordable day care for the children in her community.

ANTIDEPRESSANTS AND INDIVIDUAL THERAPY CAN BE COMBINED

Some researchers have wondered whether it is useful to combine antidepressants and individual psychotherapy. According to Hollon and his colleagues (2005), the answer is yes. Both IPT and CBT seem to be more effective in combination with antidepressants than on their own.

For instance, the combination of CBT and antidepressants is effective for 70 percent of depressed people, compared to 50 percent when either treatment is used alone.

The specific effects of each treatment are retained. Women who combine IPT with antidepressants notice quick relief from their symptoms and improved social relationships over the following year. Women who combine CBT with antidepressants have quick relief from their symptoms and increased protection from new episodes over the next two years.

COUPLE THERAPY

Because depression is associated with marital problems, a handful of studies have looked at whether couple therapy can be used to treat depression. These studies showed that couple therapy is as effective as either IPT or CBT (Gupta, Coyne, and Beach 2003). It also is as effective as antidepressants (Dessaulles, Johnson, and Denton 2003). In addition, couple therapy improves the marital relationship, a specific effect that is not seen with individual treatments.

However, some words of caution are in order. Most important, all of these studies compared individual treatments for depression with one of the two marital therapies that are known to be effective for improving marital relationships. Unfortunately, many of the therapists who practice couple therapy in the United States, Canada, the United Kingdom, and Europe do not use these therapies.

Behavioral marital therapy (BMT) (Whisman and Jacobson 1990) and emotionally focused therapy (EFT) (Johnson 1996) are known to be effective couple treatments. Both therapies have the goal of improving marital relations, but they differ in how this is achieved. BMT focuses on conflict. The therapist helps the couple stop fighting and improve the way they talk to each other to solve their problems. EFT is based on attachment theory and shares some techniques with PET. It focuses on creating a secure emotional bond between the partners. EFT therapists believe that once partners feel secure with each other, they are able to disagree and solve problems without getting into fights.

Couple therapy may not be acceptable to both partners. While a depressed woman may see a connection between her depression and her marriage, her husband is likely to blame their marital problems on her depression. Husbands of depressed women may be unwilling to commit to couple therapy as a treatment for their wives' depression. Even if they agree to start, they may find the treatment irrelevant and drop out after only a few sessions.

When is couple therapy a good choice? You need to think about the context in which your depression developed. If your marital problems began after you became depressed, you should probably try individual therapy first. Lisa is a good example. Because her emotional difficulties went back to childhood, individual therapy was a good first choice. In contrast, if your depression is a response to problems in your marriage, then couple therapy is probably a good first choice. Anne and Bill might have benefitted from couple therapy. However, like many unhappily married couples, they did not seek therapy before separating.

If you believe your relationship plays a part in your depression and your husband or partner agrees to couple therapy, this is probably a good choice for you.

Couple Therapy After Successful Individual Treatment

As depressed women get better in individual therapy, their marriages are almost always affected. How the couple responds to these changes is a critical determinant of whether the woman will become depressed again. Winnie Kung and Irene Elkin (2000) identified a group of women whose depression got better with individual treatment. About half of the women received either IPT or CBT, while the other half improved with either antidepressants or placebo. Over the following eighteen months, the women who stayed well were those whose marriages improved the most while they were being treated.

David often worried that Lisa's therapy was making her worse. Even though he tried to be supportive when he learned about the sexual abuse, he often felt attacked by her. As I described in chapter 7, Lisa's "Voice" tried to protect her by telling her David was untrustworthy. The Voice questioned everything David said and did, and she called him disparaging names. Both Lisa and David found couple therapy helpful at this point in her treatment. David needed to understand the impact sexual abuse has on a woman's intimate relationships, particularly on her ability to trust men. Lisa needed to sort out when she was justified in feeling angry with David and when she was seeing him through the lens of her abuse. Couple therapy can be helpful for women with a history of childhood sexual abuse, particularly when it occurs after good work has been done in individual therapy.

All of us create patterns in the ways we interact with the most important people in our lives. If individual therapy works, it changes those patterns, especially in romantic relationships. From the depressed woman's point of view, change is good. If she falls back into the same patterns that made her depressed in the first place, she is at risk for depression again. However, romantic partners and spouses do not always see change as positive. Sometimes they fight the new patterns their wives are trying to create. Maybe they had the power in the old relationship. Maybe they could avoid owning up to their own fears and insecurities as long as their wives felt depressed and helpless.

In my clinical experience, as women become less depressed, they become more angry and assertive. They may tell their husbands about hurts they have endured silently for years. They may demand that their husbands stop doing things they have always done or start doing things they've never done before. Change can be difficult for these husbands. They may feel unfairly attacked. They may want their "old wife" back.

VICKY, JOHN, AND THE DEPRESSION BOX

Vicky and John came to me for couple therapy. In our first session, I learned that Vicky had been successfully treated for depression in individual therapy. Through this experience, she realized she had spent a lifetime holding back her thoughts and feelings because she feared people would reject her if she told them the truth. She now told John exactly what she thought. However, they had been married for fifteen years, and John was having trouble catching up with the changes Vicky had made. John was a person with strong opinions, and he had been attracted to Vicky in part because she was "easygoing" and went along with whatever he wanted. They had no experience resolving conflict. When he and Vicky disagreed, it was war.

At the beginning of couple therapy, John claimed he wanted the "old Vicky" back. He said Vicky was being "mean" to him when she didn't agree with him or do what he wanted. Vicky was enraged. She told John he was trying to "stuff [her] back into the box" that had been her depression. She rebelled by refusing to do anything he wanted, even when he was being reasonable. For instance, she had taken an exciting new job and often worked overtime, leaving John at home with their children. Not surprisingly, John was upset by what he saw as Vicky's lack of care for him and their children. By the time they came to see me, Vicky's dilemma seemed clear to her: she could either stay married to John by getting back in her depression box or she could be herself and lose her marriage.

I empathized with both of them. I validated Vicky's need to grow and change. For years, she had been cooped up in her depression box. She wanted to spread her wings and fly. The new job was an exhilarating opportunity. But I also understood why John was afraid of the changes his wife was going through. He hadn't told Vicky he was "afraid" of her changes. Usually he criticized her and told her she was no longer a good mother, which made Vicky angry. Once I labeled John's feelings as fear, he was able to tell her he had always been afraid he loved her more than she loved him. He thought Vicky was too good for him. He was afraid that now she had more self-confidence, she would realize how smart and attractive she was and she would leave him for another man. While John was glad Vicky was no longer depressed, he was afraid of what the new Vicky might do.

Vicky was right when she accused John of trying to get her back into her box. She felt he wanted to control her. But when John expressed his fears about her changes, she realized that he tried to control her because he was afraid of losing her. She reassured him that she loved him and had no desire to leave him. She told him that she needed him to "make room" for her. It was hard for John to make room for Vicky because up to that point he had always had his way. But he said he would try. For Vicky's part, she promised to reign in her enthusiasm for her new life and remember that John needed reassurance that she loved him.

TECHNIQUES AREN'T ENOUGH

Although psychologists talk a lot about the differences between therapies, the techniques that the therapist uses in a session account for only a small part of how successful treatment is for a particular person.

The key ingredient is the client herself. She has to be ready to change, and the conditions in her life have to support her changing.

Stages of Change

About half of therapy clients drop out within the first three sessions. Many of these people were not ready to change. When people change, they go through several stages. The success of therapy is related to the stage of change they are in and how sensitive the therapist is to the process they are going through (Prochaska and Norcross 2001).

If you have read this book all the way through, you may be in the *contemplation* phase of change. You know there's a problem, but you haven't yet made a commitment to do something about it. People can stay in the contemplation stage for a long time, feeling unhappy but not seeing an obvious solution. At this stage, it is important for you to figure out why you are depressed and what you can do about it. Therapy can help, but you need to find a therapist who is willing to explore your depression with you rather than jumping in with suggestions and solutions right away or imposing his or her own point of view. PET is better suited to this phase of change than either IPT or CBT because the emphasis is on the client exploring and clarifying her feelings.

If you have tried unsuccessfully to make changes in the past year, you may be in the *preparation* phase. You may have taken "baby steps" toward change and are committed to following through with bigger changes. At this point, you need something like an experienced coach who can help you take action that will be successful.

If you are ready to change your behavior and your environment to overcome your problems, you are in the *action* phase. You have successfully changed some problematic behavior, if only for a day. You are working hard to change, and the ideal therapist for you is a kind of a consultant. The structured therapies like IPT and CBT work well for clients in these last two phases of change, and PET continues to be a good choice.

Tracy was in the preparation phase when I met her. She knew her depression was rooted in what she had experienced as a child, and she was committed to changing herself and her relationships to feel better. Our therapy sessions were focused, and she made big changes over a short period of time. Lisa was in the contemplation stage. We spent nearly twenty sessions clarifying that her depression was linked to her sexual abuse as a child. Anne was in the *precontemplation* stage. She had not connected her depression to anything about herself or her life. She only came for therapy because she was referred by her family doctor. Anne and I spent most of our time putting together the understanding that she was depressed because of her marriage to Bill.

Therapy was successful for all three women, but it took longer for Lisa and Anne than it did for Tracy. I saw Lisa for about sixty sessions over an eighteen-month period and Anne for about forty sessions over three years.

Support for Change

Change also has to be supported by the people clients love. Lisa is a good example. David believed she had been sexually abused, and he did his best to support her getting well. I saw another couple whose situation was almost identical. Sarah had been sexually abused by her father. She and her husband, Mark, came for couple therapy after he learned Sarah was having an affair with his brother. I saw Sarah alone for several sessions during which she struggled against believing her memories of sexual abuse. She was in the contemplation phase of change. When she finally got up the courage to tell Mark what she remembered, he didn't believe her. He thought she was making excuses for having an affair. He refused to go to couple therapy if she insisted she had been abused. Not longer after that, Sarah regretfully told me she was choosing her marriage over her individual therapy. If Mark had accepted what Sarah remembered, she might have been able to move into the preparation phase of change.

The Therapeutic Relationship

The client's view of her relationship with the therapist also is critical. Clients who see their therapists as warm, supportive, and accepting get better, while clients who feel criticized or misunderstood do not. You need to feel that the therapist genuinely cares for and understands you and that he or she has the skill and experience to help you. You need to feel you are working together toward a common goal—your goal, not the therapist's goal.

Therapy is an intensely personal relationship. In the same way that you cannot be friends with every person you meet, you cannot develop an intimate and mutually respectful relationship with every therapist in the phone book. In the same way that we know almost right away if we like someone, you will know quickly if the therapist is a good match for you. If you don't feel comfortable, you should talk about your feelings with the therapist to see if the two of you can work it out. Sometimes these feelings arise from simple misunderstandings. However, if talking with the therapist doesn't work, you should find someone else.

OUR LIVES DON'T CHANGE, WE CHANGE

There are a lot of treatment choices for depressed women. Antidepressant medication, interpersonal therapy, cognitive behavioral therapy, process-experiential therapy, behavioral marital therapy, and emotionally focused couple therapy are all effective treatments for depression. One may be a better choice for you than another because of your personality or particular circumstances, but they all work. However, you have to be ready to change. If you are considering getting treatment, the first question you want to ask yourself is, "Am I ready?"

Change is difficult. If you've ever tried to lose ten pounds, quit smoking, or get in shape, you know what I mean. Those changes are small compared to what you have to change so that you stop feeling depressed. But it can be done. The stories in this book are true. These clients succeeded and you can too.

Remember that our lives don't change; we change our lives.

Questions to Ask Yourself

1. Do I need to get professional help with my depression? Why? Have I been depressed before? How many times?

2. Are antidepressants for me? Do I have any concerns about taking them? How long am I willing to take them for?

3. What kind of psychotherapy would suit me best? Do I value relationships? Do I believe that good relationships can make me happy? Am I a logical person? Can I be persuaded by evidence and logical argument to change my opinions? Do I value my emotions? Does knowing what I feel help me make the right decisions?

4. Do I want a confiding relationship with a therapist, or would I prefer more of a working relationship?

5. Is my romantic relationship or marriage one of the most important sources of my depression? If I manage to change a little, do my partner's expectations of me seem to drag me back into old ways of behaving again?

6. What stage of change am I in? Can I count on other people to support my change?

references

Alexander, P. C. 1993. The differential effects of abuse characteristics and attachment in the prediction of long-term effects of sexual abuse. *Journal of Interpersonal Violence* 8:346–362.

Alpert, J. L., L. S. Brown, and C. A. Courtois. 1998. Symptomatic clients and memories of childhood abuse. *Psychology, Public Policy and the Law* 4:941–995.

Andrews, B. 1995. Bodily shame as a mediator between abusive experiences and depression. *Journal of Abnormal Psychology* 104:277–285.

Angold, A., E. J. Costello, and C. M. Worthman. 1998. Puberty and depression: The roles of age, pubertal status and pubertal timing. *Psychological Medicine* 28:51–61.

Anisman, H., and K. Matheson. 2005. Stress, depression and anhedonia: Caveats concerning animal models. *Neuroscience and Biobehavioral Reviews* 29:525–546.

Avis, N. E. 2003. Depression during the menopausal transition. *Psychology of Women Quarterly* 27:91–100.

Baumrind, D. 1989. Rearing competent children. In *Child Development Today and Tomorrow*, edited by W. Damon. San Francisco: Jossey-Bass.

Bebbington, P. 1996. The origins of sex differences in depressive disorder: Bridging the gap. *International Review of Psychiatry* 8:295–332.

Beck, A. T. 1967. *Depression: Clinical, Experimental, and Theoretical Aspects.* New York: Hoeber.

———. 1983. Cognitive therapy of depression: New perspectives. In *Treatment of Depression: Old Controversies and New Approaches*, edited by P. J. Clayton and J. E. Barrett. New York: Raven.

Beck, A. T., A. J. Rush, B. F. Shaw, and G. Emery. 1979. *Cognitive Therapy of Depression.* New York: Guilford Press.

Belsher, G., and C. G. Costello. 1988. Relapse after recovery from unipolar depression: A critical review. *Psychological Bulletin* 104:84–96.

Belsky, J., and M. Rovine. 1987. Temperament and attachment security in the strange situation: An empirical rapprochement. *Child Development* 58:787–795.

Black, D. A., R. E. Heyman, and A. M. Smith Slep. 2001. Risk factors for child physical abuse. *Aggression and Violent Behavior* 6:121–188.

Bohlin, G., B. Hagekull, and K. Andersson. 2005. Behavioral inhibition as a precursor of peer social competence in early school age: The interplay with attachment and nonparental care. *Merrill-Palmer Quarterly* 51:1–19.

Bowlby, J. 1969. *Attachment and Loss*, vol. 1, *Attachment*. New York: Basic Books.

———. 1973. *Attachment and Loss*, vol. 2, *Separation, Anxiety, and Anger*. New York: Basic Books.

———. 1980. *Attachment and Loss*, vol. 3, *Loss*. New York: Basic Books.

Brennan, P. A., C. L. Hammen, A. R. Katz, and R. M. Le Brocque. 2002. Maternal depression, paternal psychopathology, and adolescent diagnostic outcomes. *Journal of Consulting and Clinical Psychology* 70:1075–1085.

Breuer, J., and S. Freud. 1962. *Studies on Hysteria*, standard edition, vol. 2. London: Hogarth Press. (Orig. pub. 1893–1895, in German.)

Brown, G. W., and T. O. Harris. 1978. *Social Origins of Depression*. London: Free Press.

Burgess, A. W., C. R. Hartman, and T. Baker. 1995. Memory presentations of childhood sexual abuse. *Journal of Psychosocial Nursing and Mental Health Services* 33(9):9–16.

Cassidy, J., and J. Mohr. 2001. Unsolvable fear, trauma, and psychopathology: Theory, research, and clinical considerations related to disorganized attachment across the life span. *Clinical Psychology: Science and Practice* 8:275–298.

Coffey, P., H. Leitenberg, K. Henning, T. Turner, and R. T. Bennett. 1996. Mediators of the long-term impact of child sexual abuse: Perceived stigma, betrayal, powerlessness, and self-blame. *Child Abuse and Neglect* 5:447–455.

Conger, R. D., G. R. Patterson, and X. Ge. 1995. It takes two to replicate: A mediational model for the impact of parents' stress on adolescent adjustment. *Child Development* 66:80–97.

Cooper, P. J., and L. Murray. 1995. Course and recurrence of postnatal depression: Evidence for the specificity of the diagnostic concept. *British Journal of Psychiatry* 166:191–195.

Coyne, J. C., and M. M. Calarco. 1995. Effects of the experience of depression: Application of focus group and survey methodologies. *Psychiatry: Interpersonal and Biological Processes* 58:149–163.

Coyne, J. C., T. L. Schwenk, and S. Fechner-Bates. 1995. Nondetection of depression by primary care physicians reconsidered. *General Hospital Psychiatry* 17(1):3–12.

Culp, L. N., and S. R. H. Beach. 1998. Marriage and depressive symptoms: The role and bases of self-esteem differ by gender. *Psychology of Women Quarterly* 22:647–663.

Daley, S. E., and C. L. Hammen. 2002. Depressive symptoms and close relationships during the transition to adulthood: Perspectives from dysphoric women, their best friends, and their romantic partners. *Journal of Consulting and Clinical Psychology* 70:129–141.

Davies, P. T., and M. Windle. 1997. Gender-specific pathways between maternal depressive symptoms, family discord, and adolescent adjustment. *Developmental Psychology* 33:657–668.

Davila, J., T. N. Bradbury, C. L. Cohan, and S. Tochluk. 1997. Marital functioning and depressive symptoms: Evidence for a stress generation model. *Journal of Personality and Social Psychology* 73:849–861.

Dessaulles, A., S. M. Johnson, and W. H. Denton. 2003. Emotion-focused therapy for couples in the treatment of depression: A pilot study. *American Journal of Family Therapy* 31:345–353.

Dobkin, R. D., C. Panzarella, J. Fernandez, L. B. Alloy, and M. Cascardi. 2004. Adaptive inferential feedback, depressogenic inferences, and depressed mood: A laboratory study of the expanded hopelessness theory of depression. *Cognitive Therapy and Research* 28:487–509.

Feingold, A. 1994. Gender differences in personality: A meta-analysis. *Psychological Bulletin* 116:429–456.

Field, T., M. Diego, M. Hernandez-Reif, S. Schanberg, and C. Kuhn. 2002. Relative right versus left frontal EEG in neonates. *Developmental Psychobiology* 41:147–155.

Field, T., M. Diego, M. Hernandez-Reif, Y. Vera, K. Gil, S. Schanberg, C. Kuhn, and A. Gonzalez-Garcia. 2004. Prenatal maternal biochemistry predicts neonatal biochemistry. *International Journal of Neuroscience* 114:933–945.

Field, T., B. Healy, S. Goldstein, S. Perry, D. Bendell, S. Schanberg, E. A. Zimmerman, and C. Kuhn. 1988. Infants of depressed mothers show "depressed" behavior even with nondepressed adults. *Child Development* 59:1569–1579.

Gillham, J., K. J. Reivich, L. H. Jaycox, and M. E. P. Seligman. 1995. Prevention of depressive symptoms in schoolchildren: Two year follow-up. *Psychological Science* 6:343–351.

Gjerdingen, D., P. McGovern, M. Bekker, U. Lundberg, and T. Willemsen. 2000. Women's work roles and their impact on health, well-being and career: Comparisons between the United States, Sweden and The Netherlands. *Women & Health* 31(4):1–20.

Goodman, S. H., and I. H. Gotlib. 1999. Risk for psychopathology in the children of depressed mothers: A developmental model for understanding mechanisms of transmission. *Psychological Review* 106:458–490.

Gottman, J. M., L. F. Katz, and C. Hooven. 1996. Parental meta-emotion philosophy and the emotional life of families: Theoretical models and preliminary data. *Journal of Family Psychology* 10:243–268.

Gray, J. 1994. *Men are from Mars, Women are from Venus*. New York: HarperCollins.

Greenberg, L. S., L. N. Rice, and R. Elliott. 1993. *Facilitating Emotional Change: The Moment by Moment Process*. New York: Guilford Press.

Gupta, M., J. C. Coyne, and S. R. H. Beach. 2003. Couples treatment for major depression: Critique of the literature and suggestions for some different directions. *Journal of Family Therapy* 25:317–346.

Hammen, C. L. 2003. Interpersonal stress and depression in women. *Journal of Affective Disorders* 74:49–57.

Hammen, C. L., D. Burge, and C. Adrian. 1991. Timing of mother and child depression in a longitudinal study of children at risk. *Journal of Consulting and Clinical Psychology* 59:341–345.

Hammen, C. L., D. Burge, S. E. Daley, J. Davila, B. Paley, and K. D. Rudolph. 1995. Interpersonal attachment cognitions and prediction of symptomatic responses to interpersonal stress. *Journal of Abnormal Psychology* 104:436–443.

Harris, B., H. Fung, S. Johns, M. Kologlu, R. Bhatti, A. M. McGregor, C. J. Richards, and R. Hall. 1989. Transient post-partum thyroid dysfunction and postnatal depression. *Journal of Affective Disorders* 17:243–249.

Hazan, C., and P. Shaver. 1987. Romantic love conceptualized as an attachment process. *Journal of Personality and Social Psychology* 52:511–524.

Helgeson, V. S. 1994. Relation of agency and communion to well-being: Evidence and potential explanations. *Psychological Bulletin* 116:412–428.

Herman, J. L. 1992. *Trauma and Recovery*. New York: Basic Books.

Hollon, S. D., R. B. Jarrett, A. A. Nierenberg, M. E. Thase, M. Trivedi, and A. J. Rush. 2005. Psychotherapy and medication in the treatment of adult and geriatric depression: Which monotherapy or combined treatment? *Journal of Clinical Psychiatry* 66:455–468.

Hooley, J. M., and J. D. Teasdale. 1989. Predictors of relapse in unipolar depressives: Expressed emotion, marital distress, and perceived criticism. *Journal of Abnormal Psychology* 98:229–235.

Hunsley, J., C. M. Lee, and T. Aubry. 1999. Who uses psychological services in Canada? *Canadian Psychology* 40:232–240.

Jack, D. 1991. *Silencing the Self: Women and Depression*. Cambridge, MA: Harvard University Press.

Janet, P. 1907. *The Major Symptoms of Hysteria*. New York: Macmillan.

Jaycox, L. H., K. J. Reivich, J. Gillham, and M. E. P. Seligman. 1994. Prevention of depressive symptoms in school children. *Behaviour, Research and Therapy* 32:801–816.

Johnson, S. M. 1996. *The Practice of Emotionally Focused Marital Therapy: Creating Connection*. Philadelphia: Brunner/Mazel.

Johnson, S. M., J. Makinen, and J. W. Millikin. 2001. Attachment injuries in couples: A new perspective on impasses in couple therapy. *Journal of Marital and Family Therapy* 27:145–155.

Johnson, S. M., and V. E. Whiffen. 1999. Made to measure: Adapting emotionally focused couples therapy to partners' attachment styles. *Clinical Psychology: Science and Practice* 6:366–381.

Joiner, T. E., and J. Katz. 1999. Contagion of depressive symptoms and mood: Meta-analytic review and explanations from cognitive, behavioral, and interpersonal viewpoints. *Clinical Psychology: Science and Practice* 6:149–164.

Jorm, A. F. 1987. Sex and age differences in depression: A quantitative synthesis of published research. *Australian and New Zealand Journal of Psychiatry* 21:46–53.

Joyner, K., and J. R. Udry. 2000. You don't bring me anything but down: Adolescent romance and depression. *Journal of Health and Social Behavior* 41:369–391.

Judd, L. L., H. S. Akiskal, J. D. Maser, P. J. Zeller, J. Endicott, W. Coryell, M. P. Paulus, J. L. Kunovac, A. C. Leon, T. I. Mueller, J. A. Rice, and M. B. Keller. 1998. A prospective 12-year study of subsyndromal and syndromal depressive symptoms in unipolar major depressive disorders. *Archives of General Psychiatry* 55:694–700.

Kaplan, S. J., D. Pelcovitz, and V. Labruna. 1999. Child and adolescent abuse and neglect research: A review of the past 10 years. Part I: Physical and emotional abuse and neglect. *Journal of the American Academy of Child and Adolescent Psychiatry* 38:1214–1222.

Kessler, R. C. 1997. The effects of stressful life events on depression. *Annual Review of Psychology* 48:191–214.

Kim, I. J., X. Ge, G. H. Brody, R. D. Conger, F. X. Gibbons, and R. L. Simons. 2003. Parenting behaviors and the occurrence and co-occurrence of depressive symptoms and conduct problems among African American children. *Journal of Family Psychology* 17:571–583.

Klerman, G. L., M. M. Weissman, B. J. Rounsaville, and E. Chevron. 1984. *Interpersonal Psychotherapy of Depression*. New York: Basic Books.

Kobak, R., and T. Mandelbaum. 2003. Caring for the caregiver: An attachment approach to assessment and treatment of child problems. In *Attachment Processes in Couple and Family Therapy*, edited by S. M. Johnson and V. E. Whiffen. New York: Guilford Press.

Kovacs, M., and B. Devlin. 1998. Internalizing disorders in childhood. *Journal of Child Psychology and Psychiatry* 39:47–63.

Krishnakumar, A., and C. Buehler. 2000. Interparental conflict and parenting behaviors: A meta-analytic review. *Family Relations: Interdisciplinary Journal of Applied Family Studies* 49:25–44.

Kung, W. W., and I. Elkin. 2000. Marital adjustment as a predictor of outcome in individual treatment of depression. *Psychotherapy Research* 10:267–278.

Landen, M., and E. Eriksson. 2003. How does premenstrual dysphoric disorder relate to depression and anxiety disorders? *Depression and Anxiety* 17:122–129.

Leitenberg, H., L. E. Gibson, and P. L. Novy. 2004. Individual differences among undergraduate women in methods of coping with stressful events: The impact of cumulative childhood stressors and abuse. *Child Abuse and Neglect* 28:181–192.

Loftus, E. F. 2001. Imagining the past. *Psychologist* 14(11):584–587.

Lovejoy, M. C., P. A. Graczyk, E. O'Hare, E. Neuman, and G. Neuman. 2000. Maternal depression and parenting behavior: A meta-analytic review. *Clinical Psychology Review* 20:561–592.

Malarkey, W. B., J. K. Kiecolt-Glaser, D. Pearl, and R. Glaser. 1994. Hostile behavior during marital conflict alters pituitary and adrenal hormones. *Psychosomatic Medicine* 56:41–51.

Marks, M., A. Wieck, S. Checkley, and C. Kumar. 1996. How does marriage protect women with histories of affective disorder from post-partum relapse? *British Journal of Medical Psychology* 69:329–342.

Masson, J. M. 1984. *The Assault on Truth: Freud's Suppression of the Seduction Theory*. New York: Farrar, Straus and Giroux.

McLeod, J. D., R. C. Kessler, and K. R. Landis. 1992. Speed of recovery from major depressive episode in a community sample of married men and women. *Journal of Abnormal Psychology* 101:277–286.

Merikangas, K. R., M. M. Weissman, B. A. Prusoff, and K. John. 1988. Assortative mating and affective disorders: Psychopathology in offspring. *Psychiatry* 51:48–57.

Monroe, S. M., and A. D. Simons. 1991. Diathesis-stress theories in the context of life stress research: Implications for the depressive disorders. *Psychological Bulletin* 110:406–425.

Murrey, G. J., J. Bolen, N. Miller, K. Simensted, M. Robbins, and F. Truskowski. 1993. History of childhood sexual abuse in women with depressive and anxiety disorders: A comparative study. *Journal of Sex Education and Therapy* 19:13–19.

Nolen-Hoeksema, S. 1990. *Sex Differences in Depression*. Stanford, CA: Stanford University Press.

Peterson, C. 2000. The future of optimism. *American Psychologist* 55:44–55.

Prochaska, J. O., and J. C. Norcross. 2001. Stages of change. *Psychotherapy* 38:443–448.

Roberts, J. E., I. H. Gotlib, and J. D. Kassel. 1996. Adult attachment security and symptoms of depression: The mediating roles of dysfunctional attitudes and low self-esteem. *Journal of Personality and Social Psychology* 70:310–320.

Rosenstein, D. S., and H. A. Horowitz. 1996. Adolescent attachment and psychopathology. *Journal of Consulting and Clinical Psychology* 64:244–253.

Rumstein-McKean, O., and J. Hunsley. 2001. Interpersonal and family functioning of female survivors of childhood sexual abuse. *Clinical Psychology Review* 21:471–490.

Runtz, M. G., and J. R. Schallow. 1997. Social support and coping strategies as mediators of adult adjustment following childhood maltreatment. *Child Abuse and Neglect* 21:211–226.

Sarnoff, S. J. 1963. *Man Under Stress, Conference no. 7*, held at the University of California, San Francisco Medical Center.

Scott, R. L., and J. V. Cordova. 2002. The influence of adult attachment styles on the association between marital adjustment and depressive symptoms. *Journal of Family Psychology* 16:199–208.

Shirk, S. R., G. R. Gudmundsen, and R. A. Burwell. 2005. Links among attachment-related cognitions and adolescent depressive symptoms. *Journal of Clinical Child and Adolescent Psychology* 34:172–181.

Snyder, J. 1991. Discipline as a mediator of the impact of maternal stress and mood on child conduct problems. *Development and Psychopathology* 3:263–276.

Soenens, B., M. Vansteenkiste, P. Luyten, B. Duriez, and L. Goossens. 2005. Maladaptive perfectionistic self-representations: The mediational link between psychological control and adjustment. *Personality and Individual Differences* 38:487–498.

Southwick, S. M., M. Vythilingam, and D. S. Charney. 2005. The psychobiology of depression and resilience to stress: Implications for prevention and treatment. *Annual Review of Clinical Psychology* 1:255–291.

Sullivan, P. F., M. C. Neale, and K. S. Kendler. 2000. Genetic epidemiology of major depression: Review and meta-analysis. *American Journal of Psychiatry* 157:1552–1562.

Tennant, C. 2002. Life events, stress and depression: A review of the findings. *Australian and New Zealand Journal of Psychiatry* 36:173–182.

Teti, D. M., and D. M. Gelfand. 1991. Behavioral competence among mothers of infants in the first year: The mediational role of maternal self-efficacy. *Child Development* 62:918–929.

Thompson, J. M., V. E. Whiffen, and J. A. Aube. 2001. Does self-silencing link perceptions of care from parents and partners with depressive symptoms? *Journal of Social and Personal Relationships* 18:503–516.

Toth, S. L., and D. Cicchetti. 1996. Patterns of relatedness, depressive symptomatology, and perceived competence in maltreated children. *Journal of Consulting and Clinical Psychology* 64:32–41.

Trickett, P. K., and C. McBride-Chang. 1995. The developmental impact of different forms of child abuse and neglect. *Developmental Review* 15:311–337.

Van Voorhees, E., and A. Scarpa. 2004. The effects of child maltreatment on the hypothalamic-pituitary-adrenal axis. *Trauma, Violence and Abuse* 5:333–352.

Wade, T. D., and K. S. Kendler. 2000. The relationship between social support and major depression: Cross-sectional, longitudinal and genetic perspectives. *Journal of Nervous and Mental Disease* 188:251–258.

Watson, J. C., L. B. Gordon, L. Stermac, F. Kalogerakos, and P. Steckley. 2003. Comparing the effectiveness of process-experiential with cognitive-behavioral psychotherapy in the treatment of depression. *Journal of Consulting and Clinical Psychology* 71:773–781.

Whiffen, V. E. 1992. Is postpartum depression a distinct diagnosis? *Clinical Psychology Review* 12:485–508.

———. 2004. Myths and mates in childbearing depression. *Women and Therapy* 27:151–163.

———. 2005. The role of partner characteristics in attachment insecurity and depressive symptoms. *Personal Relationships* 12:407–423.

Whiffen, V. E., and J. A. Aube. 1999. Personality, interpersonal context, and depression in couples. *Journal of Social and Personal Relationships* 16:369–383.

Whiffen, V. E., and S. E. Clark. 1997. Does victimization account for sex differences in depressive symptoms? *British Journal of Clinical Psychology* 36:185–193.

Whiffen, V. E., M. E. Judd, and J. A. Aube. 1999. Intimate relationships moderate the association between childhood sexual abuse and depression. *Journal of Interpersonal Violence* 14:940–954.

Whiffen, V. E., A. V. Kallos-Lilly, and B. J. MacDonald. 2001. Depression and attachment in couples. *Cognitive Therapy and Research* 25:577–590.

Whiffen, V. E., M. A. Kerr, and V. Kallos-Lilly. 2005. Maternal depression, adult attachment and children's emotional distress. *Family Process* 44:93–103.

Whisman, M. A., and M. L. Bruce. 1999. Marital dissatisfaction and incidence of Major Depressive Episode in a community sample. *Journal of Abnormal Psychology* 108:674–678.

Whisman, M. A., and N. S. Jacobson. 1990. Brief behavioral marital therapy. In *Handbook of Brief Psychotherapies*, edited by R. A. Wells and V. J. Giannetti. New York: Plenum Press.

Wickramarantne, P., and M. M. Weissman. 1998. Onset of psychopathology in offspring by developmental phase and parental depression. *Journal of the American Academy of Child and Adolescent Psychiatry* 37:933–942.

Wilson, S. L., J. E. Kuebli, and H. M. Hughes. 2005. Patterns of maternal behavior among neglectful families: Implications for research and intervention. *Child Abuse and Neglect* 29:985–1001.

Wind, T. W., and L. Silvern. 1994. Parenting and family stress as mediators of the long-term effects of child abuse. *Child Abuse and Neglect* 18:439–453.

Young, E., and A. Korszun. 1998. Psychoneuroendocrinology of depression: Hypothalamic-pituitary-gonadal axis. *Psychiatric Clinics of North America* 21:309–323.

Valerie E. Whiffen, Ph.D., has been a researcher, professor and clinical psychologist in private practice since 1986. For twenty years, she was a professor of psychology at the University of Ottawa, where she taught students to do interpersonal therapy with depressed women and therapy with couples who are struggling with one partner's depression. She now lives near Vancouver, BC, where she is in private practice. She serves as a peer reviewer for several professional psychological journals. She has authored numerous chapters in professional books and more than forty journal articles and she is co-author of *Attachment Processes in Couple and Family Therapy* with Susan Johnson. Her primary research and clinical interests are gender and depression.

more books from new**harbinger**publications, inc.

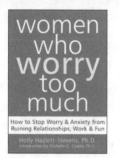

MY MOTHER, MY MIRROR

Recognizing & Making
the Most of Inherited
Self-Images

US $17.95 / ISBN: 978-1572245693

**WOMEN WHO WORRY
TOO MUCH**

How to Stop Worry & Anxiety
from Ruining Relationships,
Work & Fun

US $15.95 / ISBN: 978-1572244122

**THOUGHTS & FEELINGS,
THIRD EDITION**

Taking Control of Your
Moods & Your Life

US $21.95 / ISBN: 978-1-572245105

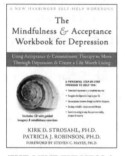

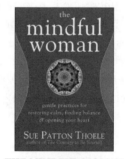

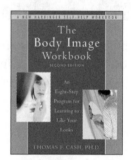

**THE MINDFULNESS &
ACCEPTANCE WORKBOOK
FOR DEPRESSION**

Using Acceptance
& Commitment Therapy to
Move Through Depression
& Create a Life Worth Living

US $21.95 / ISBN: 978-1572245488

THE MINDFUL WOMAN

Gentle Practices for
Restoring Calm, Finding
Balance & Opening Your Heart

US $15.95 / ISBN: 978-1572245426

**THE BODY IMAGE
WORKBOOK,
SECOND EDITION**

An Eight-Step Program
for Learning to Like Your Looks

US $19.95 / ISBN: 978-1572245464

available from

new**harbinger**publications, inc.

and fine booksellers everywhere

To order, call toll free **1-800-748-6273**

or visit our online bookstore at **www.newharbinger.com**

(VISA, MC, AMEX / prices subject to change without notice)